Access to History

General Editor: Keith Randell

Germany: The Third Reich, 1933–45

Geoff Layton

Hodder & Stoughton

LONDON SYDNEY AUCKLAND

The cover illustration is a German poster of Adolf Hitler, produced in 1938 (Courtesy Bundesarchiv, Koblenz)

Some other titles in the series:

The Unification of Italy 1815–70
Andrina Stiles
ISBN 0 340 51809 X

The Unification of Germany 1815–90
Andrina Stiles
ISBN 0 340 51810 3

Russia 1815–81
Russell Sherman
ISBN 0 340 54789 8

Rivalry and Accord: International Relations 1870–1914
John Lowe
ISBN 0 340 51806 5

Reaction and Revolutions: Russia 1881–1924
Michael Lynch
ISBN 0 340 53336 6

Stalin and Khrushchev: The USSR 1924–64
Michael Lynch
ISBN 0 340 52559 2

Italy: Liberalism and Fascism 1870–1945
Mark Robson
ISBN 0 340 54548 8

British Library Cataloguing in Publication Data
Layton, Geoff
  Germany: Third Reich, 1933–45. – (Access
  to History Series)
  I. Title II. Series
  943.086

  ISBN 0–340–53847–3

First published 1992
Impression number 10 9 8 7 6 5 4 3
Year   1998 1997 1996 1995 1994 1993

© 1992 Geoff Layton

Typeset by Wearset, Boldon, Tyne and Wear
Printed in Great Britain for the educational publishing division of Hodder & Stoughton Ltd, Mill Road, Dunton Green, Sevenoaks, Kent by Page Bros, Norwich.

Contents

Preface

To the general reader

Although the *Access to History* series has been designed with the needs of students studying the subject at higher examination levels very much in mind, it also has a great deal to offer the general reader. The main body of the text (i.e. ignoring the Study Guides at the ends of chapters) forms a readable and yet stimulating survey of a coherent topic as studied by historians. However, each author's aim has not merely been to provide a clear explanation of what happened in the past (to interest and inform): it has also been assumed that most readers wish to be stimulated into thinking further about the topic and to form opinions of their own about the significance of the events that are described and discussed (to be challenged). Thus, although no prior knowledge of the topic is expected on the reader's part, she or he is treated as an intelligent and thinking person throughout. The author tends to share ideas and possibilities with the reader, rather than passing on numbers of so-called 'historical truths'.

To the student reader

There are many ways in which the series can be used by students studying History at a higher level. It will, therefore, be worthwhile thinking about your own study strategy before you start your work on this book. Obviously, your strategy will vary depending on the aim you have in mind, and the time for study that is available to you.

If, for example, you want to acquire a general overview of the topic in the shortest possible time, the following approach will probably be the most effective:

1 Read chapter 1 and think about its contents.
2 Read the 'Making notes' section at the end of chapter 2 and decide whether it is necessary for you to read this chapter.
3 If it is, read the chapter, stopping at each heading or ★ to note down the main points that have been made.
4 Repeat stage 2 (and stage 3 where appropriate) for all the other chapters.

If, however, your aim is to gain a thorough grasp of the topic, taking however much time is necessary to do so, you may benefit from carrying out the same procedure with each chapter, as follows:

1 Read the chapter as fast as you can, and preferably at one sitting.
2 Study the flow diagram at the end of the chapter, ensuring that you understand the general 'shape' of what you have just read.

3   Read the 'Making notes' section (and the 'Answering essay questions' section, if there is one) and decide what further work you need to do on the chapter. In particularly important sections of the book, this will involve reading the chapter a second time and stopping at each heading and * to think about (and to write a summary of) what you have just read.

4   Attempt the 'Source-based questions' section. It will sometimes be sufficient to think through your answers, but additional understanding will often be gained by forcing yourself to write them down.

When you have finished the main chapters of the book, study the 'Further Reading' section and decide what additional reading (if any) you will do on the topic.

This book has been designed to help make your studies both enjoyable and successful. If you can think of ways in which this could have been done more effectively, please write to tell me. In the meantime, I hope that you will gain greatly from your study of History.

Keith Randell

Acknowledgements

The Publishers would like to thank the following for permission to reproduce illustrations:

Bundesarchiv, cover.
The Imperial War Museum, London p. 35.
Collection of Akron Art Museum, Museum Acquisition Fund p. 39.
Polish Institute and Sikorski Museum p. 94.
Edimedia p. 107.

Every effort has been made to trace the copyright holders of the pictures reproduced on pages 67 and 110. Any rights not acknowledged here will be acknowledged in subsequent printings if notice is given to the publishers.

CHAPTER 1

The Third Reich – An Introduction

1 Whatever one may think of his [Hitler's] methods – and they are
certainly not those of a parliamentary country – there can be no
doubt that he has achieved a marvellous transformation in the
spirit of the people, in their attitude towards each other, and in
5 their social and economic outlook ... As to his popularity,
especially among the youth of Germany, there can be no manner
of doubt. The old trust him; the young idolise him. It is not the
admiration accorded to a popular leader. It is the worship of a
national hero who has saved his country from utter despondency
10 and degradation ... He is the George Washington of Germany
... On the other hand, those who imagine that Germany has
swung back to its old Imperialist temper cannot have any
understanding of the character of the change. The idea of
Germany intimidating Europe with a threat that its irresistible
15 army might march across frontiers forms no part of the new
vision. What Hitler said at Nuremburg is true. The Germans will
resist to the death every invader of their own country, but they no
longer have the desire themselves to invade any other land.

These words were written in 1937, not by a Nazi, not even by a Nazi
sympathiser, but by a Welshman, a Liberal and a former British prime
minister – David Lloyd George. Of course, numerous contemporary
assessments of Hitler's Germany were published and they ranged
widely from fulsome praise to outraged contempt. Yet, since 1945 when
the grim reality of Nazism had become apparent, eulogies for the Third
Reich have essentially remained the preserve of politically motivated
right-wing extremists. Indeed, there is probably no other regime in
history which has been so universally condemned by serious academic
scholarship. However, despite such unanimity, there is certainly no
modern-day consensus when it comes to explaining Nazism – quite the
reverse. The Third Reich has become one of the most controversial
fields of historical study in the world, for it has not only generated the
usual kinds of dispute over points of analysis and interpretation: it has
also raised issues of morality and philosophy which have brought into
question the very nature of the historian's craft.

1 The Historical Issues

As with so many of history's great controversies, it is the questions of
causation and definition which have prompted the most vigorous
debate. How and why were the Nazis able to gain power and why was it

possible to create and maintain a regime of such brutality? What exactly was Nazism and what did it represent?

At the very centre of all these questions stands the figure of Hitler himself. For some, the 'Hitler factor' provides reassuring proof that history unfolds as the result of the power, influence and actions of the individual. In this sense Hitler can be seen as one of the 'great men' of history (albeit in the evil category). A leader, comparable to Julius Caesar or Napoleon Bonaparte, who created a powerful political movement, directed his nation's affairs according to his will and then led the world into the most destructive military conflict ever. Many eminent historians maintain the basic validity of a Hitler-centred interpretation of the Third Reich, and they are described as belonging to the 'intentionalist' school. Cynics might argue that the 'intentionalist' interpretation is rather convenient, since it allows much of the blame for the crimes of Nazism to be directed towards a dead *Führer*. However, there is plenty of historical research to support the idea that the personal role of Hitler has been greatly over-emphasised. Historians of the 'structuralist' school have played down the significance of Hitler and his intentions and have instead focused their attention on the structure of the Third Reich in its broadest sense. In particular, they have examined the apparatus of Party and state in order to identify the political complexities of the regime and its decision-making processes. For the student approaching the subject of the Third Reich it is, of course, impossible to ignore the position of Hitler. However, it is vitally important to avoid being drawn automatically into a Hitler-centred analysis. His power and influence must be assessed: it must not be automatically assumed.

Although this book deals almost exclusively with Germany, it should not be forgotten that the Third Reich coincided with a number of other regimes which have been labelled 'fascist' and/or 'totalitarian'. This has led some historians (and more particularly political scientists) to portray Nazism as the German example of a common type of mid-twentieth century political movement. Left-wing analysts, for example, have traditionally favoured 'generic' interpretations of fascism, which have emphasised the vital importance of economic forces and the class alignments within capitalist societies to explain the emergence of fascist systems of government. However, the explanation of Nazism as merely a variety of fascism carries with it many far-reaching implications. In particular, it raises the possibility that Nazism was not a historical phenomenon which resulted from a unique set of circumstances and that its roots were not necessarily Germanic, let alone purely Hitlerian. Likewise, the application of the term 'totalitarian' to the Third Reich has been favoured by more liberal historians who have sought to underline the similarities between left and right-wing one-party states. According to such a view, Nazism could not only be compared to contemporary regimes such as that of Mussolini's Italy and Stalin's

Russia, but also to the post-war people's republics of eastern Europe. Clearly, the Third Reich should not be studied in isolation and so it is important to compare and contrast the history of Germany with developments in Italy, Spain and the USSR. However, one must avoid the temptation of forcing the Third Reich to conform to certain predetermined political models. The European context must be borne in mind, whilst allowing for the particular circumstances which permitted the development of National Socialism in Germany.

Those historians who have not wished to explore the implications of such parallels have tended to emphasise Nazi racial and foreign policy as its most distinguishing features of uniqueness. According to such a view, the importance placed by the Nazis on their racial ideology, which in turn provided the justification for their expansionist programme of conquest and domination, sets it apart from all other regimes. And certainly, the grandiose nature of Nazi imperial ambitions, together with the brutal and clinical implementation of the racial 'new order', have been vital factors in making the Third Reich the focus of such attention. The attempted genocide of the Jews, the resettlement and murder of millions of other 'inferior' people, and the bloodshed wrought on Germany's own people, are happenings which not only require rational historical analysis, but also arouse questions about the nature of mankind and of morality.

A further controversial issue relating to the Third Reich involves an assessment of the extent of its 'revolutionary' character. This has been a point of heated debate amongst historians for many years. For some, Nazism is viewed as an abhorrent aberration, which clearly marked a fundamental change of direction in Germany's evolutionary path. For others, it came to represent the natural culmination of developments within Germany since the middle of the nineteenth century. This question of continuity and change in German history is central to any understanding, explanation and definition of the Third Reich. However, in order to appreciate its subtleties, it is necessary to place the Third Reich in the context of recent German history.

2 The Historical Context

In 1871, in the wake of the Franco-Prussian War, the German Empire was proclaimed. For the first time in their history the states of Germany had been formally unified. 74 years later, amidst the ruins of its major cities, Hitler's Third Reich surrendered to the Allied forces, thus ushering in a division of Germany which took political form in the creation of two separate German states in 1949 and which lasted for more than 40 years.

From its inception, the Second Reich (now referred to as the *Kaiserreich* by historians) bore both the stamp of its creator, Bismarck, and of the circumstances of its creation. It deliberately excluded

German Catholic Austria. Its federal constitution, by making concessions to provincial feelings, also allowed for the domination of Prussia,
which was by far the strongest of all the federal states. Moreover, the
King of Prussia was also *Kaiser* (Emperor) of Germany and his powers
were immense: he alone chose the Imperial Chancellor; he ultimately
decided matters of foreign policy; and he was Supreme Commander of
the combined armed forces of the Empire. Thus, despite the existence
of an imperial parliament, the *Reichstag*, and a federal council, there
was no disguising the fact that effective power lay with the *Kaiser* and
his chosen chancellor. Whilst Wilhelm I (1871–88) and Chancellor
Bismarck worked in tandem the system was able to work moderately
well, but the coronation of Wilhelm II (1888–1918) ushered in a new
and more uncertain era, which highlighted a number of inherent
weaknesses in the political arrangements of the Empire. Wilhelm II's
own personal failings of character made him unsuited to the direction of
affairs of state, so that despite the lofty ideals and the great plans there
was never any real degree of consistency in policy-making. Constitutional problems were further exacerbated by developments in the
German economy and society. Industrialisation had not only made
Germany the strongest economy on the continent, but it had also
inevitably wrought fundamental changes in the structural balance of
society. The rise of an entrepreneurial middle class and a large working
class were clearly a threat to the established social order. By 1914 the
Social Democrats, as the representatives of the working classes, had
become by far the largest party in the *Reichstag* and yet, the powers of
the *Reichstag* remained strictly limited by the terms of the constitutional arrangements made in 1871. As a result, on the eve of the First World
War, Germany was still governed by a quasi-autocracy bolstered by a
number of conservative interest groups, or elites. The most significant
of these were the army, the bureaucracy and the *Junkers* (the large
landowners).

Whether Germany could have evolved peacefully into some kind of
constitutional democracy remains open to debate, but there can be little
doubt that the strains and resentments generated by total war during
1914–18 not only caused the demise of the *Kaiserreich* in the revolution
at the end of 1918, but also contributed decisively to the political
developments of the next 15 years.

The Weimar Republic, which replaced the *Kaiserreich*, was flawed
from the moment of its birth. It was the product of military defeat and
the social distress caused by war and, in this sense, its creation was a
'knee-jerk' reaction to a crisis, rather than the result of a genuine desire
for fundamental change. Moreover, it meant that subsequently democratic parties were associated with national humiliation, which gave
currency to the myth of the 'stab in the back' – the idea that the
politicians had betrayed the country by surrendering when the army
could still have won the war. This situation was in turn greatly

exacerbated by the imposition of the Treaty of Versailles, since the new republic was saddled with the responsibility of accepting the unacceptable. Even the new constitution, drawn up with such careful consideration, ended up as a series of compromises between the forces of revolution and reaction, which allowed the survival of traditional vested interests while also advancing sophisticated democratic procedures and principles. Unfortunately for the republic, the newly created institutions did not always show the expected loyalty to the constitution, nor sufficient commitment to the values of an open pluralist democracy.

By the time of the first *Reichstag* election in June 1920, the changing popular mood was clear, as 35 per cent of the electorate supported non-democratic parties of either the extreme left or right. From 1920 Weimar 'democracy' veered between weak short-lived cabinets and authoritarian government by means of the president's emergency powers. The republic managed to overcome the Kapp Putsch of 1920 (an attempted *coup* by army officers supported by conservative nationalists). It even survived the much greater crises of 1923 – the French occupation of the Ruhr and the 'Great Inflation', which rendered money absolutely worthless. However, the implications of such episodes for the long-term survival of democracy were profound: the loyalty of the army to the republic was uncertain; public confidence had been hit hard by the inflation; the German economy was in a weakened state and subject to international forces; and powerful militaristic and nationalist groups had made clear their intention to destroy the regime.

Even in the period of so-called prosperity and stability from 1924 to 1929 it was impossible to disguise the fundamental political weakness. Coalition governments (often without a majority in the *Reichstag*) came and went with alarming regularity, and were often only created after considerable intrigue and compromise. Field Marshall Hindenburg, who was known to have little sympathy for the regime, was elected President in 1925 – a post he was not prepared to accept until he had gained the permission of the ex-*Kaiser*!

When the depression finally brought economic ruin to Weimar Germany it created an environment in which anti-republican forces could excel. Thus in the years 1930–3, as the number of voters sympathetic to democracy declined, so did the chance of saving the young republic. Germany was already a semi-dictatorship from September 1930. By 1932 only 43 per cent of the electorate voted in the July *Reichstag* elections for pro-republican parties. In the light of this evidence, it is difficult to escape the conclusion that Weimar-style democracy was unlikely to survive. This, of course, is not to argue that the establishment of the Nazi regime in 1933 was a natural consequence.

Naturally, one would expect to find aspects of continuity and change in the history of Germany between 1871 and 1945. The really crucial historical task is to decide where the overall emphasis lies between the two. So, although the aim of this book is to explore some of the most significant issues concerning National Socialism in Germany, it is important always to be aware of the historical background of the Third Reich. In particular, the following themes need to be seen within this broader sweep of German history: the nature of the political structure and the part played by the key interest groups within it; the importance attached to certain political and social attitudes, especially racism, anti-democracy and anti-socialism; and finally the vital issue of Germany's position in the international arena. In this way, it should be possible to come to an informed provisional judgement about whether the Third Reich represents the final phase in a continuity based upon the military-state structure founded in 1871, or whether it marks a revolutionary break with the traditions of Germany's previous history.

3 The Problems of Historical Interpretation

In November 1989 the Berlin Wall, the symbol of post-war divided Germany, came down and one year later Germany once again became a unified state. Such dramatic developments underlined the truth behind the maxim that history is always a product of the time in which it is written. The reunification of Germany had seemed an impossibility only months previously. Until that moment historians had naturally based their analyses of German history on the perspective of a clearly divided Germany, which seemed to suggest that the period of unity from 1871–1945 was merely a 'blip' in the long-term tradition of division and disunity.

Our historical perspective is rarely static for very long. This is particularly the case with the history of the Third Reich, which has developed into one of the great historiographical debates of the last 40 years. The steady stream of new books and articles on the subject shows no sign of drying up. This to some extent reflects the huge range of archives available on this topic – a source-base which continues to grow as more and more material is released by the authorities. The sheer volume of evidence clearly presents the historian of the Third Reich with very different problems to those faced by those who are researching a much earlier period of German history. Even so, historians are rarely satisfied with the available evidence. They always want more. And so the knowledge that a wealth of material was destroyed – either deliberately or as a result of the war – is a cause of considerable frustration. The revelation of the so-called 'Hitler diaries' (later shown to be fakes) in the 1980s created such excitement amongst academic historians mainly because it raised the possibility of explaining the nature of Nazi government, which to a large extent still remains shrouded in uncertainty.

However, the controversies surrounding the Third Reich go much deeper than differences over the interpretation of evidence, as was recently revealed by the state of 'open warfare' which developed within Germany's academic community. The Third Reich became the focus of a vitriolic debate, which was soon dubbed the *Historikerstreit* (historians' dispute), although its waves reverberated well beyond university walls. At the heart of this dispute lay the fundamental problems facing any student studying the Third Reich. How do you interpret rationally and objectively a subject clouded by the horrors of the holocaust? Secondly, is it possible to 'historicise' (consider in a true historical fashion) the Third Reich as a normal period of history? And finally, specifically for the German student, there remains the problem of having to come to terms with the Nazi past as part of one's own national identity.

Almost inevitably as the Third Reich recedes into the past the increased time-gap creates a certain detachment which allows for greater objectivity. Yet, even after so many years, some people would still argue that 'this repellant subject' (G. Mann) is too loaded with political and moral overtones for the normal standards of historical analysis and interpretation to apply. Therein, perhaps, lies an explanation of why the subject continues to be the focus of such interest for both historian and student. The Third Reich is a particularly daunting intellectual challenge, but it is one which cannot be ignored.

Making notes on 'The Third Reich – An Introduction'

In making notes on this introductory chapter your aim should be to assure yourself that you have identified and understood the main issues and problems raised by the debate. It is important for you to keep these in mind as you read the rest of the book.

Write brief answers to the following questions:

1 Why is it so difficult to treat the Third Reich as a normal period of history?
2 What do you understand by the term 'continuity and change' in the context of German history 1871–1945? What are the implications of viewing the Third Reich as part of a continuity? What are the implications of viewing it as marking a fundamental change?
3 What are the major areas of historical controversy among historians of the Third Reich?

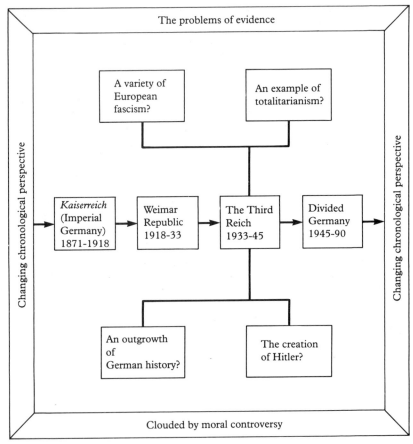

Summary – Introduction

Studying the Third Reich

The Third Reich is likely to be a central topic in any examination course on twentieth-century European or world history. It is very rare indeed for examiners not to set questions on the subject, so you can feel confident that your efforts in studying this topic will not be wasted. However, it is a very large topic, as is shown by the fact that one whole volume in this series is devoted to it. Despite this, it really does need to be studied in conjunction with several other main-stream themes:

1 The development of German history in the 70 years before 1933, and especially the failure of the Weimar Republic.
2 The other dictatorships in inter-war Europe, and especially Stalin's Russia and Mussolini's Italy.

3 International relations 1919–45, with particular reference to the origins of the Second World War.

Therefore, it would be very unwise to study the Third Reich in isolation or, particularly, to concentrate on just one or two aspects of the topic.

Hopefully, your reading and note-taking of the first chapter has allowed you to identify the problems of interpretation and the major issues of historical controversy. You need to keep these in mind as you work on the rest of this book, as they will help you to come to your own general conclusions about the Third Reich – this is the purpose behind chapter 8. However, before that point is reached, you will need to study and think about some of the more specific issues of historical significance. These are:

1 The rise of National Socialism – chapters 2–3 (this must also be dovetailed with your study of the Weimar Republic and why it failed).
2 The establishment and structure of the regime – chapters 4–5.
3 The impact of the Third Reich on society – chapter 6.
4 The significance of Nazi foreign policy – chapter 7 (this must also be related directly to your study of international relations).

Note. All German words and phrases are translated and explained in the glossary on pages 152–153.

CHAPTER 2

Hitler and the Nazi Party

1 Germany and the World Depression – The Socio-Economic Impact

The primary task of any historian is to interpret the past from the available evidence. Such an analysis inevitably involves the division of history into periods, and the obvious identification of key turning-points. In the history of the Weimar Republic, October 1929 seems to stand out clearly as one such turning-point because of two decisive events. Firstly, Gustav Stresemann died, thus robbing the young democracy of the only statesman who could perhaps have handled a major crisis. Stresemann had been Weimar's only democratic politician of stature to emerge: his chancellorship had helped to overcome the crises of 1923 and, as Foreign Minister from 1923–9, he had successfully negotiated Germany's rehabilitation in the international community. Secondly, the New York Stock Exchange on Wall Street collapsed, which brought about a major economic depression throughout the world.

However, it must be remembered that weaknesses in the German economy existed well before these two vital happenings of October 1929. The prosperity of 1924–9 had been built on very insecure foundations, since both German industry and German agriculture had borrowed extensively from the United States at high rates of interest. Moreover, many of these loans were short-term, which meant that repayment could be demanded with only limited warning. If the American creditors were to lose confidence, then the collapse of the German economy would be almost unavoidable.

Indeed, the agricultural sector of the economy was already in recession before 1929. World food prices fell by 30 per cent between 1925 and 1929 because of over-production, and German farmers were faced with the potentially disastrous combination of high rents for their land and lower prices for their produce. Another section of society to feel the economic pinch at this time was the *Mittelstand*, made up of small-scale retailers and self-employed artisans. They found it increasingly difficult to survive in an economic environment dominated by the wealth and influence of big business and mass trades unions. They particularly resented the cost of the new welfare measures, which had to be paid for out of increased taxation and social security contributions. It is therefore clear that behind the image of prosperity and boom associated with 1924–9, Germany's economy was far from healthy. By 1928 economic growth was slowing down, and unemployment already stood at 1.3 million 18 months before the dramatic events of October 1929.

* The First World War had witnessed a dramatic shift in the financial and economic balance of power from Europe to America. The United States had become the world's strongest economy and Wall Street had assumed the role of the leading stock exchange. One major result of this pre-eminence was that the United States provided money, in the form of loans and capital investment, to virtually all countries of the world. Throughout the 1920s American confidence in its economic potential fuelled a massive economic boom. The American economy had grown by 70 per cent between 1913 and 1929. In Germany the equivalent figure was 4 per cent. In this atmosphere even shares were bought 'on the margin', which meant that the purchaser paid only a fraction of the price and then gambled on prices continuing to rise so as to make a profit and repay debts. When eventually over-confidence began to give way to doubts because of figures showing a decline in production, some major investors sold their shares. The effect was to create a wave of panic selling on Black Thursday, 24 October 1929. In the next few months prices spiralled downwards ruining speculators, brokers and many bankers.

However, the Wall Street Crash did not only affect the financial community in the United States. Its repercussions were to be felt throughout the world, and Germany was probably more susceptible to its consequences than any other country. Almost immediately the loans and investment dried up and this was soon followed by demands for the repayment of those loans which had been advanced so willingly over the previous five years. At the same time, the Crash precipitated a further decline in the prices of food and raw materials, as industrialised nations reduced their imports. But the knock-on effects of this action rebounded upon the more advanced economies, since many primary producers could no longer afford to import manufactured goods. World trade slumped as demand collapsed. In this situation German industry could no longer pay its way. Unsupported by loans and with diminished export markets, prices and wages fell whilst the number of bankruptcies increased. During the winter of 1929–30 unemployment rose above 2 million. Only 12 months after the Crash, it had reached 3 million. By September 1932 it stood at 5.1 million. It peaked in early 1933, when 6.1 million Germans were unemployed. Germany was faced with yet another major economic and social crisis, only a few years after the trauma of the 'Great Inflation'.

* Economic statistics are a vital source for the historian of the modern world. Yet, on their own they can provide only a limited understanding of an event such as the Depression. The unemployment figures, for example, do not take into account those who never registered. Nor do they recognise the extent of short-time working throughout German

industry. Above all, such statistics fail to convey the extent of the human consequences of this disaster.

The Depression in Germany was all pervasive; few families escaped its detrimental effects. Many manual workers, both skilled and unskilled, faced the prospect of indefinite unemployment. For their wives there was the impossible task of trying to feed families and keep homes warm on the money provided by paltry social security benefits. However, such problems were not to be limited to the working class: this depression also dragged down the middle classes. From the small-scale shopkeepers to the graduate professionals in law and medicine, people struggled to survive in a world where their goods and services were decreasingly in demand. For such casualties the decline in their economic position was further accentuated by the loss of pride and respectability, which accompanied poverty and unemployment. In the countryside the situation was no better than in the towns. As world demand contracted further, the agricultural depression deepened markedly, leading to widespread rural poverty. For some tenant farmers there was even the ultimate ignominy of eviction from tenancies which had been in their families for generations.

In the relative prosperity of today it is difficult to appreciate the scale of the economic and social suffering which struck Germany in the early 1930s. To many ordinary respectable Germans it must have seemed as if society itself was breaking down uncontrollably. One-third of the population was on the dole; the city of Cologne could not pay the interest on its debts; banks closed their doors; in Berlin large crowds of unemployed youngsters were kept occupied with open-air games of chess and cards! In such a situation it is perhaps not surprising that people lost faith in the Weimar Republic, which seemed to offer no end to the misery, and saw salvation in the solutions offered by political extremism.

2 Germany and the World Depression – The Political Impact

In 1929 the German government was in the hands of Hermann Müller's Grand Coalition, which had been formed after the general election of May 1928. Yet, at the very time when unity and firm government were required to tackle the economic crisis, the Weimar Republic was being torn apart by the resurrection of the emotive issue of reparations.

The Dawes Plan (1924) had successfully overcome the reparations crisis of the early 1920s by rescheduling payments based on Germany's capacity to pay, but from the outset it had been seen as a temporary measure until Germany regained its economic strength. In early 1929 the IARC (Inter-Allied Reparations Commission) formed a committee of international financiers under the chairmanship of the American banker Owen Young. Its report in June 1929 suggested a new scheme of payments. Germany was to continue paying reparations until 1988, but the final sum was reduced to £1,850 million (only one-quarter of the figure demanded in 1921). After some negotiation, during which Stresemann procured an Allied promise to evacuate the Rhineland by June 1930, the Young Plan was accepted.

However, in right-wing circles, Stresemann's achievement was seen as yet another betrayal of German interests to the Allies. In their view any payment of reparations was based upon the 'lie' of Germany's war guilt (Article 231 of the Treaty of Versailles) and therefore the new scheme had to be opposed. A national committee, led by the new leader of the Nationalists, Alfred Hugenberg, was formed to fight the Young Plan. Hugenberg was also Germany's greatest media tycoon. He owned 150 newspapers and a publishing house, as well as the world famous UFA film organisation. He now used all his resources to promote his message. Moreover, he generated support from a wide variety of right wing factions – the *Stahlhelm* (the largest ex-servicemen's organisation), the Pan-German League, leading industrialists and Hitler's Nazis. Together this 'National Opposition' drafted a *Law against the Enslavement of the German People* which denounced any payment of reparations and demanded the punishment of any minister agreeing to such a treaty. The proposal gained enough signatures for it to be made the issue of a national referendum in December 1929. In the end the 'National Opposition' won only 5.8 million votes, a long way short of the 21 million required by the constitution for success. However, the campaign had stirred nationalist emotions and focused opposition on the democratic government at a vital time. It had also brought together many right-wing opponents of the Republic and, perhaps most important of all for the future, it had given Hitler and the Nazis a national standing for the first time.

Müller's government successfully withstood the attack from the 'National Opposition'. However, it was not so resilient to its own internal divisions. Müller, a Social Democrat, struggled to hold the coalition together, but both the People's Party, since the death of Stresemann, and the Centre Party, since the resignation of its leader Marx in 1928, had drifted to the right. Not surprisingly, it was an issue of government finance which finally brought down the government in March 1930. The sharp increase in unemployment had created a large deficit in the insurance scheme, and the Social Democrats and the People's Party could not reconcile their differences on how to tackle it. The Social Democrats, as the political representatives of the trades unions, wanted to increase the contributions and to maintain the levels of welfare payments. The People's Party, on the other hand, had strong ties with big business and insisted on reducing benefits. Müller had no option but to tender the resignation of his government.

President Hindenburg appointed Heinrich Brüning as the new Chancellor. At first sight this appeared an obvious choice, since he was the parliamentary leader of the Centre Party, the second largest party in the *Reichstag*. However, with hindsight, it seems clear that Brüning's elevation marked the end of true parliamentary government, for he was manoeuvred into office by the select circle of political intriguers who now surrounded the ageing President. Otto Meissner, the President's State Secretary, Oskar von Hindenburg, the President's son, and Major General Kurt von Schleicher, the political voice of the army, had all lost faith in the democratic process. Instead, they looked to the President and the emergency powers of Article 48 of the constitution as a means of creating an authoritarian government backed by the army. In Brüning they saw a respectable conservative figure, who also believed in the necessity of firm leadership. Initially he hoped to achieve this by heading a centre-right coalition, which excluded the Social Democrats.

Brüning's response to the growing economic crisis was to propose cuts in government expenditure, so as to achieve a balanced budget and avoid any risk of re-kindling inflation. It was rejected in the *Reichstag* by 256 votes to 193 in July 1930. In this situation Brüning put the proposals into effect by means of an emergency decree signed by the President according to Article 48. The *Reichstag* challenged the legality of this action and voted for the withdrawal of the decree. Deadlock had been reached. Brüning therefore asked Hindenburg to dissolve the *Reichstag* and to call an election for September 1930. He was hopeful that in the developing crisis the electorate would be encouraged to back his centre-right coalition. The election results proved him wrong. The real beneficiary was the Nazi Party, which increased its vote from 810,000 to a staggering 6,409,600.

3 Hitler's Early Years

The election of 1930 had catapaulted the Nazis to the forefront of German politics. It had transformed the Party's leader into a politician of national significance. Yet, there had been little in the background of Adolf Hitler (1889–1945) to suggest that he would become a powerful political figure.

Hitler was born at Braunau-am-Inn in 1889 in what was then the Austro-Hungarian Empire. He failed to impress at school, and after the death of his parents he moved to Vienna in 1907. There he applied unsuccessfully for a place as a student at the Academy of Fine Arts. For the next six years he led an aimless and unhappy existence in the poorer districts of the city. It was not until he joined the Bavarian Regiment on the outbreak of war in 1914 that he found a real purpose in life. He served bravely throughout the war, and was awarded the Iron Cross 1st Class. When the war ended he was in hospital recovering from a British gas attack. By the time he had returned to Bavaria in early 1919 he had already framed in his mind the core of what was to become National Socialism: a fervent German nationalism; a hatred of democracy and socialism; a rabid anti-semitism; and a racially inspired view of society and its values, the *Volksgemeinschaft* (see pages 20 and 86).

Such a mixture of ideas in a man whose personal life was also much of a mystery – he had no close family and few real friends – has excited 'psycho-historians' to extraordinary speculation. Did his anti-semitism originate from contracting syphillis from a Jewish prostitute? Could his authoritarian disposition be explained by his upbringing at the hands of an old and repressive father? Such psychological diagnoses – and there are many – may interest the student, but the supporting evidence for such explanations is at best flimsy. As a result, the conclusions reached are highly speculative and do not really help to explain the key question of how and why Hitler became such an influential political force.

It was because of his entrenched right-wing attitudes that Hitler was employed in the politically charged atmosphere of 1919 as a kind of spy by the political department of the army's Bavarian section. One of his investigations brought him into contact with the DAP (*Deutsche Arbeiterpartei* – German Workers' Party) which was not a movement of the revolutionary left, as Hitler had assumed on hearing its name, but one committed to nationalism, anti-semitism and anti-capitalism. Hitler joined the tiny party and immediately became a member of its committee. His energy, oratory and propaganda skills soon made an impact on the small group, and it was Hitler who with the party's founder, Anton Drexler, drew up the party's 25 point programme in February 1920. At the same time it was agreed to change the party's name to the NSDAP, the National Socialist German Workers' Party.

GERMAN WORKERS PARTY ——> NSDAP

1 We demand the union of all Germans in a Greater Germany on the basis of the right of national self-determination.

2 We demand equality of rights for the German People in its dealings with other nations, and the revocation of the peace
5 treaties of Versailles and Saint Germain.

3 We demand land and territory (colonies) to feed our people and to settle our surplus population.

4 Only members of the *Volk* (nation) may be citizens of the State. Only those of German blood, whatever their creed may
10 be members of the nation. Accordingly no Jew may be a member of the nation.

7 We demand that the State shall make it its primary duty to provide a livelihood for its citizens. If it should prove impossible to feed the entire population, non-citizens must be
15 deported from the Reich.

10 It must be the first duty of every citizen to perform physical or mental work. The activities of the individual must not clash with the general interest, but must proceed within the framework of the community and be for the general good.

20 11 We demand therefore the abolition of incomes unearned by work.

14 We demand profit-sharing in large industrial enterprises.
15 We demand the extensive development of insurance for old
    age.
25 18 We demand the ruthless prosecution of those whose activities
    are injurious to the common interest. Common criminals,
    usurers, profiteers must be punished with death, whatever
    their creed or race
22 We demand the abolition of the mercenary army and the
30   formation of a people's army.
23 We demand legal warfare on deliberate political mendacity
    and its dissemination in the press.

(For an analysis of Nazi ideology see page 19.)

By mid-1921 it was clear that Hitler was the driving-force behind the party, although he still only held the post of propaganda chief. It was his powerful speeches which had impressed local audiences and had helped increase party membership to 3,300. He had encouraged the creation of the armed squads to protect party meetings. It was his development of early propaganda techniques – the Nazi salute, the swastika, the uniforms – which had done so much to give the party a clear and easily recognisable identity. Alarmed by Hitler's increasing domination of the party, Drexler and some other members of the committee tried to curtail his influence. In the ensuing power struggle Hitler soon mobilised support and at two meetings in July 1921 he won sufficient support to become chairman and *Führer* (leader) of the party.

Having gained supreme control over the party in Munich, Hitler aimed to subordinate the other 45 semi-autonomous branches to his leadership. To a large extent this was achieved within Bavaria in the years 1921–3, but it proved impossible with those groups further afield. This period also witnessed the staging of the first party rally and the development of the armed squads into an organised group – the SA (*Sturm Abteilung* – Stormtroopers).

4 The Beer-Hall *Putsch*, 1923

The successful take-over of power by Mussolini in Italy in October 1922, combined with the developing internal crisis in Germany, convinced Hitler that the opportunity to seize power had arrived. But the Nazis were far too weak on their own to stage any kind of political take-over. It was the need of allies which led Hitler into negotiations with the Bavarian State Government and the Bavarian section of the army during 1923.

The government of the State of Bavaria was led by the ultra-conservative Gustav von Kahr, who blamed most of Germany's problems on the socialist dominated government in Berlin. Like Hitler he wished to destroy the Republican regime, although his long-term aim was the creation of an independent Bavaria. By October 1923 General von Lossow, the army's commander in Bavaria, had fallen under von Kahr's spell and had even begun to disobey orders from the Defence Minister.

It was with these two men that Hitler plotted to 'March on Berlin' in the style of Mussolini's coup. However, at the eleventh hour, von Kahr and von Lossow, fearing failure, decided to abandon the plan. Hitler was not so cautious and preferred to press on rather than lose the opportunity. On 8 November, when von Kahr was addressing a large audience in one of Munich's beer halls, Hitler and the Nazis took control of the meeting and declared a 'national revolution'. Drama soon turned into farce. Hitler had insufficient support from the army and police, and the attempted take-over of Munich was easily crushed. Fourteen Nazis were killed and Hitler himself was arrested on a charge of treason.

Despite the inglorious result, Hitler gained much political advantage from the episode. He won the respect of many other right-wing nationalists for having had the courage to act and he turned his trial into a propaganda success both for himself and for the Nazi cause. Indeed his sentence of five years (the minimum stipulated by the Weimar Constitution and actually reduced to ten months) seemed like an act of encouragement on the part of the judiciary.

5 The Ideology of National Socialism

Nazism always emphasised the importance of action over thought. However, whilst in Landsberg prison, Hitler dictated the first part of *Mein Kampf* (My Struggle) which in the following years became the bible of National Socialism. Together with the 25-point programme of 1920, it provides the basic framework of Hitler's ideology and, by extension, of Nazism itself.

Hitler's ideas were built upon his concept of race. He believed that humanity consisted of a graduated hierarchy of races and that life was no more than 'the survival of the fittest'. He argued that Social Darwinism necessitated a struggle between races, just as animals fought for food and territory in the wild. Furthermore, he considered it vital to maintain racial purity, so that the strong would not be undermined by the blood of the weak.

It was a crude philosophy, which appears even more simplistic when Hitler's analysis of the races is considered. The *Herrenvolk* (master-race) was the Aryan race, made up of the peoples of Northern Europe and epitomised by the Germans. It was the task of the Aryan to remain pure and to subjugate the inferior races. At the lower end of his racial pyramid Hitler placed the Negroes, the Slavs, the Gypsies and, the particular focus of his hatred, the Jews. Hitler's anti-semitism was violent and irrational. The Jew became the universal scapegoat for the

Nazis, responsible for all the problems of Germany past and present. Hitler saw the Jewish community as a kind of cancer within the German body politic – a disease that had to be treated, as the following extract from *Mein Kampf* illustrates:

> 1 The adulteration of the blood and racial deterioration conditioned thereby are the only causes that account for the decline of ancient civilizations; for it is never by war that nations are ruined, but by the loss of their powers of resistance, which are exclusively a
> 5 characteristic of pure racial blood. In this world everything that is not of sound stock is like chaff. Every historical event in the world is nothing more nor less than a manifestation of the instinct of racial self-preservation, whether for weal or woe.

A number of points in the 1920 programme demanded socialist reforms, and for a long time there existed a faction within the party which emphasised the anti-capitalist aspect of Nazism. Hitler accepted these points in the early years because he recognised their popular appeal, but he himself never showed any real commitment to such ideas, and they were to be dropped after he came to power. What Hitler did promote was the concept of the *Volksgemeinschaft* (people's community). This remained the vaguest element of the Nazi ideology, and is therefore difficult to define precisely. It meant working together for the benefit of the nation; the provision of jobs and social benefits; and the encouragement of 'German values'. Such a system could of course only benefit those who belonged to the German *Volk* and who willingly accepted the loss of individual freedoms in an authoritarian system.

In Hitler's opinion there was no realistic alternative to strong dictatorial government. Ever since his years in Vienna he had viewed parliamentary democracy as weak and ineffective. It went against the German historical traditions of militarism and absolutism, and furthermore it encouraged the development of an even greater evil, communism. More specifically, Hitler saw Weimar democracy as a betrayal. In his eyes, it was the democratic and socialist politicians of 1918, 'the November Criminals', who had stabbed the German army in the back, by accepting the armistice and establishing the Republic. Since then Germany had lurched from crisis to crisis. In place of democracy Hitler envisaged the creation of an all-embracing one party state that would be run on the leadership principle (*Führerprinzip*). Thus, the mass of individuals in society were to be subjugated for the common good, but the individual leader was to be elevated in order to rouse the nation into action, and to take the necessary decisions.

The final element in Nazi ideology was an aggressive nationalism, which developed out of the particular circumstances of Germany's recent history. The armistice of 1918 and the subsequent Treaty of Versailles had to be overturned, and the lost territories had to be restored to Germany. But Hitler's nationalism called for more than a mere restoration of the 1914 frontiers. It meant the creation of an empire (*Reich*) to include all those members of the German *Volk* who lived beyond the frontiers of the Kaiser's Germany: the Austrian Germans, the Sudeten Germans, the German communities along the Baltic coast, all were to be included within the borders of Germany. Yet, Hitler's nationalist aims did not end there. He dreamed of a Greater Germany, a superpower, capable of competing with the British Empire and the United States. Such an objective could be achieved only by territorial expansion on a grand scale. This was the basis of Hitler's demand for *Lebensraum* (living-space) for Germany. Only by the conquest of Poland, the Ukraine and Russia could Germany obtain the raw materials, cheap labour and food supplies so necessary for continental supremacy. The creation of his 'New Order' in eastern Europe also held one other great attraction: namely, it would involve the destruction of Russia, the centre of world communism. As he argued in *Mein Kampf*:

1 The German people must be assured the territorial area which is necessary for it to exist on earth . . . People of the same blood should be in the same *Reich*. The German people will have no right to engage in a colonial policy until they shall have brought
5 all their children together in one state. When the territory of the *Reich* embraces all the Germans and finds itself unable to assure them a livelihood, only then can the moral right arise, from the need of the people, to acquire foreign territory. The plough is then the sword; and the tears of war will produce the daily bread
10 for the generations to come . . . In the future our people will not obtain territory, and therewith the means of existence, as a favour from any other people, but will have to win it by the power of a triumphant sword . . .
    The right to territory may become a duty when a great nation
15 seems destined to go under unless its territory be extended. And this is particularly true when the nation in question is not some little group of negro people but the Germanic mother of all the life which has given cultural shape to the modern world. Germany will either become a World Power or will not continue to exist at
20 all . . . The future goal of our foreign policy ought to be an Eastern policy which will have in view the acquisition of such territory as is necessary for our German people. To carry out this policy we need the force which the mortal enemy of our nation, France, now deprives us of.

To describe Hitler's thinking as an ideology is really to flatter it. It lacked coherence and was intellectually superficial and simplistic. It was not even a rational system of thought. It was merely a collection of ideas not very cleverly pieced together. Although the combination was unique, it was not in any positive sense original. Every aspect of Hitler's thinking was to be found in the nationalist and racist writings of the nineteenth century. His nationalism was an outgrowth of the fervour generated in Germany in the years between Prussia's struggle against Napoleon and the unification of 1871. His idea of an all-German *Reich* was a simple repetition of the demands for the 'Greater Germany' made by those German nationalists who criticised Bismarck's limited unification. Even the imperialism of *Lebensraum* had already found expression in the programme of 'Germanisation' supported by those writers who saw the German race as somehow superior. This growing veneration for the *Volk* had also gone hand-in-hand with the development of racist ideas, and in particular of anti-semitism. Thus, even before Hitler and other leading Nazis were born, the core of what would become Nazism was already current in political circles. It was to be found in the cheap and vulgar pamphlets sold to the masses in the large cities; in the political programme of respectable pressure groups, such as the Pan-German League; within the corridors of Germany's great universities; and in the creative works of certain cultural figures such as the composer Richard Wagner. However, despite these close links, one must avoid labelling Nazi ideology as the logical result of Germany's intellectual legacy. It is all too easy to search out those elements which prove the linkage theory whilst ignoring the host of other evidence which points to entirely different intellectual traditions – and there were many in the case of Germany. Moreover, it is well to remember that a number of countries, but especially Britain and France, also witnessed the propagation of very similar ideas at this time. In that sense nationalism and racism were an outgrowth of nineteenth-century European history. Nazi ideology may not have been original, but it should not therefore be assumed that it was an inevitable result of Germany's past.

6 The Creation of a Party Structure

In Landsberg prison Hitler reflected on the failure of the 1923 *Putsch*. He concluded that an armed coup was no longer an appropriate tactic and that the only sure way to succeed was to work within the Weimar Constitution and to gain power by legal means. Such a policy of legality would necessitate the creation of a party structure geared to gaining success at the ballot box.

However, when Hitler left prison in December 1924 the future looked bleak. The party was in disarray: its leading members were split into factions and the membership was in decline. More significantly, the atmosphere of crisis which had prevailed in the early years of the republic had given way to a period of political and economic calm. The party was officially refounded on 27 February 1925, but it was a party deeply divided in a number of ways. Not everyone agreed with the new policy of legality. Traditional regional hostilities, particularly between Catholic Bavaria and Protestant Prussia, continued to exist. Most importantly, policy differences had emerged between the nationalist and anti-capitalist wings of the party. For over a year Hitler struggled with this internal friction, until eventually in February 1926, at a special party conference in Bamberg, he mobilised sufficient support to re-establish his supremacy. The Nazi Party was to be run according to the *Führerprinzip* (leadership principle). There was to be no place for the discussion of differences.

The most significant development in the years before the Depression lay in the reorganisation of the party structure. The whole of Germany was divided into regions (*Gaue*), which reflected the electoral geography of Weimar's system of proportional representation. The control of each region was placed in the hands of a *Gauleiter*, who then had the responsibility of creating district (*Kreis*) and branch (*Ort*) groups. In this way a vertical party structure was created throughout Germany, which did not detract from Hitler's own position of authority as leader. At the same time a number of new Nazi organisations were founded: the SS, an elite body of black-shirted guards, sworn to absolute obedience to the Führer; the Hitler Youth, to attract the support of the young; and the Nazi Teachers' Association. The party was taking shape and its membership was increasing: 27,000 in 1925, 49,000 in 1926, and 72,000 in 1927. Moreover, it had successfully taken over most of the other right-wing racist groups in Germany. Such progress, however, could not compensate for the disappointment of the election in May 1928, when the Party won only 2.6 per cent of the vote and a mere 12 seats in the *Reichstag*. It seemed as if the improvement in the party's organisation and the policy of legality had failed to bring political success.

7 Electoral Breakthrough

Although the overall result of the 1928 election was poor for the Nazis, it hid considerable regional variations. In some rural areas, especially in the north-west, they had polled over 10 per cent of the vote. The onset of the agricultural depression in the previous couple of years had created a more receptive climate for Nazi agitation there. The point was not lost on the Nazi leaders, who deliberately started to direct their propaganda at rural and middle-class audiences.

In political terms, 1929 was initially dominated by the controversial Young Plan and the referendum organised by Hugenberg (see page 15). For Hitler, the Nazi involvement in this campaign brought rich rewards. It opened up the treasure-trove of Hugenberg's media empire to Nazi propaganda. Nazism was made respectable by its association with conservative nationalists. In addition, some leading industrialists, such as Emil Kirdorf, the great coal magnate from the Ruhr, and Fritz Thyssen, the steel manufacturer, were sufficiently impressed by Hitler to make financial contributions to the party. Hitler thought that such advantages far outweighed the defeat of the referendum proposal, and by the end of the year there was confirmation of a Nazi political advance. The membership had shot up to 178,000 and there had been steady gains for the party in state elections. In Thuringia, for example, its share of the vote had increased to 11.3 per cent and a leading party figure, Wilhelm Frick, had accepted a key post in the state government.

As the Depression began to take hold of Germany in the course of 1930, the Nazi agitation gained increasing public sympathy. But no one – not even Hitler – had expected the dramatic result of the *Reichstag* election in September of that year (see page 16). With 107 seats, the Nazis had become the second largest political party in Germany. This was achieved partly at the expense of the Nationalists, whose vote was halved, and partly by the decline of the middle-class democratic parties, the Democrats and the People's Party, who lost 20 seats between them. Nazi success, however, cannot just be explained by these 'protest votes'. It has been estimated that nearly half of the Nazi seats were won by the party attracting new voters. The electorate had grown by 1.8 million since the previous election, and the turn-out had increased from 76.5 per cent to 82 per cent. It would seem that the Nazis had not only picked up a fair proportion of these young first-time voters, but had also persuaded many people, who had previously not participated in elections to support their cause.

Only one other party had reason to celebrate the election results of September 1930 – the Communist Party. It increased its share of the vote to 14.3 per cent, mainly at the expense of the Social Democrats, and thereby won a further 23 seats. The overall implications for the supporters of democracy were therefore alarming, for 39.6 per cent of the voting public had supported non-democratic parties. The drift towards political extremism was well and truly under way.

DEMOCRACY   BECOMING   ABOLISHED

Making notes on 'Hitler and the Nazi Party'

As you read this chapter (and the next one) you should be continually aware that it raises issues which originate much earlier than 1929. This applies particularly to the question of Weimar's problems and also to that of Nazism's ideological roots in German history.

Sections 1 and 2 highlight the impact of the Depression in Germany. However, it would be a good idea to find out from other books how the Depression affected other countries. In this way you should be able to appreciate the extent of Germany's problems.

Sections 3 and 4 provide background and, although it is not

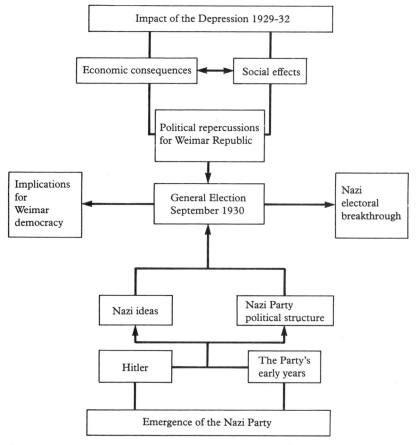

Summary – Hitler and the Nazi Party

necessary to note the finer detail, you should try to appreciate the insight given into Hitler the individual.

Sections 5 and 6 are very different in terms of content, but they need to be well noted, since a knowledge of Nazi organisation and ideology are vital to a good understanding of the topic.

Section 7 brings together the two strands of the chapter whilst acting as a link to chapter 3.

The following headings, sub-headings and questions should provide a suitable framework for your notes:

1 Germany and the World Depression – The Socio-economic Impact

1.1 The German economy on the eve of the Depression.

1.2 The 'Wall Street Crash' and its economic consequences. Why was the German economy so badly hit?

1.3 The social effects.

2   Germany and the World Depression – The Political Impact

2.1 The immediate political repercussions in 1929–30. How significant was the problem of reparations in the developing crisis of 1929–30?

3   Hitler's Early Years

3.1 Construct a simple dateline of his background and career, 1889–1922.

4   The Beer-hall Putsch, 1923

4.1 What is the significance of the beer-hall putsch?

5   The Ideology of National Socialism

5.1 Racism.

5.2 The people's community.

5.3 Dictatorship.

5.4 Nationalism.

5.5 How original was Nazi ideology?

6   The Creation of a Party Structure, 1925–9

6.1 The structure of the Nazi Party.

6.2 Why was this so significant?

7   Electoral Breakthrough 1929–30

7.1 The extent of Nazi success.

7.2 Is the onset of the Depression a sufficient explanation of Nazi electoral popularity?

Source-based questions on 'Hitler and the Nazi Party'

1 The Nazi Party 25-point Programme of 1920

Carefully read the extracts from the programme on pages 17 and 18. Answer the following questions:

a) Explain in your own words what the Nazis meant by the word *Volk*. (2 marks)

b) Which of the points do you consider to be 'socialist'? Explain your answer in each case. (8 marks)

c) In what ways does the Party programme attempt to appeal to the fears and prejudices of the German people? (5 marks)

d) What are the strengths and weaknesses of the extract as evidence of Nazi political intentions? (5 marks)

2 Hitler's *Mein Kampf*

Carefully read the extracts from *Mein Kampf* on pages 20 and 21. Answer the following questions:

a) Explain what Hitler meant by i) 'the force which France now deprives us of' (line 25), and ii) 'the plough is then the sword' (line 8). **(4 marks)**

b) From these two extracts what do you consider to have been Hitler's strongest political emotion? Explain your answer. **(5 marks)**

c) On the basis of these two extracts, what do you consider to have been the strengths and weaknesses of *Mein Kampf* as a piece of political propaganda? **(7 marks)**

d) Hitler's policies on race and foreign affairs are reasonably clear. Why do you think so many contemporaries chose to ignore the implications of *Mein Kampf*? **(4 marks)**

CHAPTER 3

The Nazi Road to Power, 1930–3

1 Semi-dictatorship

The decision of Heinrich Brüning to call the election of September 1930 has been a focus of controversy over the years. For some historians it was a naive action, taken before all the other options had been exhausted. Others have been more sympathetic and have seen Brüning as a victim of circumstances who was forced into the decision by the lack of co-operation from other parties, particularly the Social Democrats. But wherever the responsibility lies, Brüning's political position after the election appeared very difficult. His plan of reinforcing his parliamentary support from the centre-right had not succeeded. Instead, he faced the uncompromising opposition of the more powerful extremes of left and right.

However, Brüning was not unseated as Chancellor. He still enjoyed the support of Hindenburg and the Social Democrats decided to 'tolerate' his use of Article 48 (though not to join his government) because of the threat now facing the republic from the extremists. In this way true parliamentary democracy gave way to presidential government with a degree of backing from the *Reichstag*.

Brüning's aim over the next two years was to undermine the extreme nationalists by a combination of his economic and foreign policies. By pursuing the strong deflationary programme, he hoped to demonstrate to the Allies that the payment of reparations was no longer possible. In this he succeeded, for reparations were eventually abolished by the Lausanne Conference of June 1932 – ironically a few days after Brüning's resignation. Similarly, he pursued the idea of the Austro-German Customs Union, partly as a sop to nationalist desires for the *Anschluss* (the union of Germany and Austria), but also to encourage a revival in trade. But the announcement of such a scheme in March 1931 backfired badly. France referred the proposal to the International Court of Justice on the grounds that it was contrary to the terms of the Treaty of Versailles, and the judges supported France's objection by eight votes to seven. This was a major blow for Brüning and his Foreign Minister, Curtius, felt compelled to resign. Finally, he aimed to achieve international recognition for Germany's right to equality of armaments at the long-heralded Disarmament Conference which opened in February 1932.

However, not only did Brüning's policy fail to bring him any political benefits, it also did nothing to curb the economic and social crisis at home. In June 1931 one of Germany's major banks, the Danat, closed its doors to customers. By early 1932 unemployment had topped 5 million. Increasingly, political tensions were played out in the streets where the private political armies clashed. In addition, confidence in Brüning was beginning to wane among the clique which surrounded President Hindenburg.

Brüning's last act was to secure the re-election of President Hindenburg whose first seven year term of office came to an end in the spring of 1932. He had initially tried to secure an extension of two years, so as to avoid further political disruption at such a troubled time, but a constitutional amendment of this kind required a two-thirds majority in the *Reichstag*, and both the Nazis and the Nationalists refused to co-operate. The 84-year-old President reluctantly agreed to stand again, and this time he was opposed by Hitler.

The Nazis fought a very effective campaign, but it was Hindenburg who won. He polled 19.3 million votes (53 per cent), Hitler 13.4 million (36.8 per cent) and Thälmann, the Communist, 3.7 million (10.2 per cent). However, it was a negative victory. Hindenburg had only been elected because the alternatives were too frightening. Moreover, there was no certainty that he had either the ability or the desire to stand by the democratic constitution. On the other hand, Hitler, despite losing, had doubled the Nazi vote and had projected a powerful personal image.

Hindenburg showed no gratitude to Brüning for supporting his re-election. At the end of May 1932 the President forced his Chancellor's resignation by refusing to sign any more emergency decrees. It is generally agreed that this decision had been prompted by the group surrounding the old man. Schleicher, recognising Brüning's failures, had become convinced that the Nazis could no longer be ignored and must be included as part of a more right-wing government which did not rely on the 'toleration' of the Social Democrats. The President finally succumbed to this line of argument when news broke of Brüning's latest economic proposal to deploy 600,000 unemployed workers on Junker estates in East Prussia. Such a plan was portrayed as 'agrarian bolshevism' in landowning circles, and it provided the perfect opportunity for Schleicher to engineer Brüning's fall.

Brüning was an honest, hard-working and honourable man who failed. The extent to which this failure should be seen as his responsibility, and how much as the result of circumstances and forces beyond his control, is a matter for conjecture. But there is little doubt about its significance, because it led to the dubious appointment of Franz von Papen as Chancellor.

The new Chancellor had been suggested to Hindenburg by Schleicher. As an aristocrat Papen had good connections with high society, and as a Catholic he was a member of the Centre Party, although his political views mirrored those of the Nationalists. Such 'virtues' quickly formed the basis for a close friendship between Hindenburg and Papen. Papen was also politically ambitious, but his understanding and experience of politics was limited (he did not even hold a seat in the *Reichstag*!). If the choice of Papen was greeted with incredulity by many, it was the man's very lack of expertise which appealed to Schleicher, who saw the opportunity to influence events more directly through him. The new cabinet, soon nicknamed the 'Cabinet of Barons', was dominated by aristocratic landowners and industrialists. However, Schleicher had also extracted a promise from Hitler that the Nazis would not oppose the new government in return for two concessions: the dissolution of the *Reichstag* and the calling of fresh elections; and the ending of a government ban on the SA and SS, which had been introduced in the wake of violence during the presidential campaign. In this way Schleicher hoped to achieve his objective of a right-wing authoritarian government with a measure of popular support in the form of the Nazis. The *Reichstag* was therefore dissolved, and an election was arranged to take place on 31 July 1932.

The campaign which followed the announcement of the election was brutal, as street violence once again took hold in the large cities. In the month of July alone 86 people died as a result of political fights. Such bloodshed provided Schleicher and Papen with the excuse to abolish the state government of Prussia on 20 July on the grounds of its ineffectiveness. The coalition of Centre and Social Democrats there had been a focus of right-wing resentment since 1919, but it was now removed by Papen simply declaring a state of emergency and appointing himself Reich Commissioner of Prussia. This was an arbitrary and unconstitutional act, and yet the Social Democrats (and the trades unions) gave in without opposition. Whether resistance would have achieved anything is debatable, but their passive response is indicative of the extent to which the forces of democracy had lost the initiative.

Many on the right wing congratulated Papen on the Prussian *coup d'etat*. However, it does not seem to have won him any additional electoral support. When the election results came in, it was again the Nazis who had cause to celebrate. They had polled 13.7 million votes and had won 230 seats. Hitler was the leader of by far the largest party in Germany and constitutionally he had every right to form a government.

2 Nazi Voters

The point is often made that Hitler and the Nazis never gained an overall majority in *Reichstag* elections. However, such an occurrence was unlikely because of the number of political parties in Weimar Germany and the operation of the proportional representation system. Considering this, Nazi electoral achievements by July 1932 were quite staggering. The 13,745,000 voters who had supported them represented 37.4 per cent of the electorate, thus making Hitler's party the largest in the *Reichstag*. Only one other party on one other occasion had polled more – the SPD in the revolutionary atmosphere of January

1919. Nazism had become a mass movement with which millions identified, and as such it laid the foundations for Hitler's coming to power in January 1933. Who were these Nazi voters and why were they attracted to the Nazi cause?

It has already been suggested that the Nazis won more support from new voters and previous non-voters than from other parties, and this trend was to continue until March 1933. However, such an explanation is insufficient on its own. A study of Table 1 reveals a number of features.

Table 1			
The rise of the Nazi vote in *Reichstag* elections in relation to other political groups. Percentage of the vote gained by each party.			
Reichstag Election	20.5.28	14.9.30	31.7.32
Nazi Party	2.6	18.3	37.3
Protestant middle-class parties			
– Nationalist Party	14.2	7.0	5.9
– People's Party	8.7	4.5	1.2
– Democratic Party	4.8	3.8	1.0
Business Party	4.9	4.0	0.3
Others	9.2	10.0	2.3
TOTAL	41.8	29.3	11.8
Catholic parties			
– Centre Party and Bavarian People's Party	15.2	14.8	15.0
Left-wing parties			
– Social Democratic Party	29.8	24.5	21.6
– Communist Party	10.6	13.1	14.3
TOTAL	40.4	37.6	35.9

It seems fairly clear that the Nazis made extensive gains from those parties with a middle-class and/or a Protestant identity. However, it is also apparent that the Catholic parties, the Communist Party and, to a large extent, the Social Democrats were able to withstand the Nazi advances. This therefore raises the interesting question of why these three parties managed to retain the allegiance of their supporters, while the others so obviously failed.

Geographically, Nazi support was higher in the north and east of the country and lower in the south and west. Right across the North

German Plain, from East Prussia to Schleswig-Holstein, the Nazis gained their best results and this seems to reflect the significance of two important factors – religion and the degree of urbanisation. In those areas where Catholicism predominated, the Nazi breakthrough was less marked, whereas the more Protestant regions were more likely to vote Nazi. Likewise, the Nazis fared less well in the large industrial cities, but gained greater support in the more rural communities. Consequently, the Nazi vote was at its lowest in the Catholic cities of the west, such as Cologne and Düsseldorf. It was at its highest in the Protestant countryside of the north and north-west, such as Schleswig-Holstein and Pomerania. Ironically, therefore, Bavaria, a strongly Catholic region, and the birth-place of Nazism, had one of the lowest Nazi votes in Germany.

Such a picture does not of course take into account the exceptions created by local circumstances. For instance, the border area of Silesia was mainly Catholic and urbanised, and yet it recorded a very high Nazi vote (probably the result of nationalist passions generated in a border province which had lost half its land to Poland) Moreover, such an analysis should not obscure the fact that the Nazis still boasted a broader cross-section of supporters than any other party. At this time 32.5 per cent of party members could be classified as workers. The point was made in a recent study of voting habits that the Nazis only became a mass party by making some inroads into the working-class vote. Hitler therefore succeeded in appealing to all sections of German society – it is simply that those from Protestant, rural and middle-class backgrounds sympathised in greater numbers. Why was this?

Firstly, both Catholicism and socialism represented well-established ideologies in their own right and both opposed Nazism on an intellectual level. Secondly, the organisational strength of each movement provided an effective counter to Nazi propaganda: for socialism there was the trades union structure; for Catholicism there was the Church hierarchy, extending right down to the local parish priest. Thirdly, both movements had been attacked during the Second Reich and, as so often happens, persecution had resulted in a strengthening of group identity. It was therefore much harder for the Nazis to break down the traditional loyalties of working-class and Catholic communities. On the other hand, the Protestants and middle classes were not so tied. Indeed, what appears to have been common to many of the Nazi voters was a lack of faith in and identity with the existing system, and a belief that their traditional role and status in society was under threat. This, in essence, is the view of the political scientist, Seymour Lipset, who sees fascism in general as middle-class radicalism – 'the extremism of the centre'. It is supported by many historians of Nazism. This kind of sociological interpretation also tends to substantiate the view that ideologically Nazism successfully portrayed itself as both revolutionary and reactionary, since it wished to destroy the republic while at the

same time promising a return to a glorious bygone age. For the
shopkeepers, craftsmen, farmers, white collar workers and many
professional people, the crisis of 1929–33 was merely the climax of a
series of disasters since 1918. Hitler was therefore able to exploit what
has been called 'the politics of anxiety'. He seemed able to offer to many
Germans an escape from overwhelming crisis and a return to respectability.

Another clearly identifiable group of Nazi sympathisers was the
youth of Germany. The Depression hit at the moment when youngsters
from the pre-war baby-boom came of age. However good their
qualifications were, they had little chance of finding work. 41.3 per cent
of those who became party members before 1933 had been born
between 1904 and 1913 – although that age group represented only 25.3
per cent of the total population. Thus it was the young who filled the
ranks of the SA. Often unemployed, disillusioned and without hope for
the future, many youngsters saw Nazism as a movement for change.
And the SA activities gave them something to do!

It is possible therefore to come to some tentative conclusions about
who voted for the Nazis and perhaps why. However, statistics may be
presented and interpreted in a variety of ways, while sociological
explanations can easily degenerate into simplistic generalisations which
fail to take into account the widely differing views that existed.
Consequently, it is important for the history student to consider such
analyses in a critical fashion and to treat their conclusions with caution.

3 Nazi Political Methods

MAIN form OF PROPAGANDA
WAS MASS
RALLIES

FIGURES DON'T TAKE
INTO ACCOUNT
OPPOSING VIEWS

Even so, it would be naive to assume that voters for the Nazi Party were
simply won over by the appeal of a radical political ideology at a time of
economic crisis. There were numerous other fringe parties on the
extreme right which publicised similar messages. What differentiated
the Nazis and ensured that it was them the voters chose was their
revolutionary political style or, to use present-day jargon, the presentation and packaging of the party and its programme.

From his earliest days in politics Hitler had shown an uncanny but
cynical awareness of the power of propaganda. In 1924 in *Mein Kampf*
he had written:

1 The receptive powers of the masses are very restricted, and their
understanding is feeble. On the other hand, they quickly forget.
Such being the case, all effective propaganda must be confined to
a few bare essentials and those must be expressed as far as
5 possible in stereotyped formulas. These slogans should be persis-
tently repeated until the very last individual has come to grasp the
idea that has been put forward.

Such ideas were to remain the basis of Nazi propaganda, and there can be little doubt that their implementation in the years 1929–33 played a vital part in Nazi success.

The whole process of Nazi propaganda was highly organised. From April 1930 Joseph Goebbels was put in charge of a propaganda machine which reached right down to branch level. In this way information and instructions could be sent out from party headquarters and adapted to local circumstances. It also allowed the party to target its money and efforts on the key electoral districts. Finally, it encouraged feed-back from the grass-roots, so that particularly effective ideas could be put into practice elsewhere.

Above all, it was the range of propaganda techniques and their increasingly sophisticated application which marked a new approach in electioneering. Posters and leaflets had always played an important role, but now the electorate was deluged with them. The Nazis practised mass politics on a grand scale, whilst showing a subtlety and an understanding of psychology which we now associate with advertising agencies. The following directive was issued by the Reich Propaganda Department to all *Gau* Propaganda Departments during the presidential campaign of 1932:

> 1 . . . Hitler Poster. The Hitler poster depicts a fascinating Hitler head on a completely black background. Subtitle: white on black – 'Hitler'. In accordance with the Führer's wish this poster is to be put up only during the final days (of the campaign). Since
> 5 experience shows that during the final days there is a variety of coloured posters, this poster with its completely black background will contrast with all the others and will produce a tremendous effect on the masses . . .

Modern technology was also beginning to be exploited. Loudspeakers, radio, film and records were all used. Expensive cars and aeroplanes were hired, not only for the practical purpose of transporting Hitler quickly to as many places as possible, but also to project a statesman-like image. In 1932 three major speaking programmes were organised for Hitler called 'Flight over Germany'. At a local level the political message was projected by the Party arranging social events and entertainments – sports, concerts, fairs.

However, it was perhaps in the organisation of the mass rallies that the Nazis showed their mastery of propaganda. The intention was to create an atmosphere so emotional that all members of the crowd would succumb to the collective will. This is the idea of 'mass suggestion' and every kind of device was used to heighten the effect: uniforms, torches, music, salutes, flags, songs and anthems, and speeches from leading personalities. Many people have since described how they were converted as a result of such meetings.

Nazi Party election poster – 'Our last hope: Hitler'

Yet, although the Nazis went to great lengths to emphasise national unity – by exploiting foreign policy issues above all – they also correctly recognised the need to direct propaganda according to people's social and economic interests. Specific leaflets were produced for different social groups, and Nazi speakers paid particular attention to the worries and concerns of the individual clubs and societies they addressed. In this way the Nazi propaganda message was tailored to fit a whole range of people; farmers, workers, the unemployed, shopkeepers and businessmen all came to see National Socialism in a slightly different way.

There was one other strand to this Nazi revolution in political style: the systematic encouragement and use of violence. Weimar politics had been a bloody affair from the start, but the growth of the SA and SS unleashed an unprecedented wave of violence, persecution and intimidation. During the campaign of July 1932, there were 461 political riots in Prussia alone; battles between Communists and Nazis on 10 July left 10 dead; a week later 19 died after the Nazis marched through a working-class suburb of Hamburg. Such activities were encouraged by the Nazi leadership, as control of the streets was seen as vital to the expansion of Nazi power. The ballot box of democracy remained merely a means to an end, and therefore other non-democratic tactics were considered legitimate in the quest for power. The Nazis poured scorn on rational discussion and fair play. For them the end did justify the means. For their democratic opponents, there was the dilemma of how to resist those who exploited the freedoms of a democratic society merely to undermine it.

4 The Appointment of Hitler as Chancellor

The political strength of the Nazi Party following the July elections was beyond doubt. However, there still remained the problem for Hitler of how to translate this popular following into real power. He was determined to take nothing less than the post of Chancellor for himself. This was unacceptable to both Schleicher and Papen, who were keen to have Nazis in the cabinet but only in positions of limited power. Therefore, the meeting between Hitler, Papen and Hindenburg on 13 August ended in deadlock. While Papen retained the sympathy of Hindenburg, Hitler's ambitions would remain frustrated.

Noakes describes the period from August to December 1932 as 'the months of crisis' for the Nazis, since 'it appeared the policy of legality had led to a cul-de-sac'. Party morale declined and some of the wilder SA elements became increasingly restless. Papen, on the other hand, grew confident that the political stalemate was undermining the position of the Nazis, who, he believed, had reached the zenith of their electoral support (an opinion shared by the British ambassador). Consequently, he dissolved the new *Reichstag* when it met on 12

September. In many respects Papen's reading of the situation was sound. The Nazis were short of money, their morale was low and the electorate was growing tired of all the elections. These factors undoubtedly contributed to the fall in the Nazi vote on 6 November to 11.7 million (33.1 per cent), which gave them 196 seats. However, Papen's tactics had not achieved their desired end, since the fundamental problem of overcoming the lack of majority *Reichstag* support for his cabinet remained. Hitler stood firm – he would not join the government except as Chancellor.

In his frustration, Papen began to consider a drastic alternative; the dissolution of the *Reichstag*, the declaration of martial law and the establishment of a presidential dictatorship. However, such a plan was anathema to Schleicher who found Papen's growing self-confidence, as well as his friendship with President Hindenburg, additional causes for concern. Schleicher still believed that the popular support of the Nazis could not be ignored, and that Papen's plan would give rise to civil commotion. When he informed Hindenburg of the army's lack of confidence in Papen, the President was forced unwillingly to demand the resignation of his friendly Chancellor.

Schleicher at last came out into the open, and on 2 December Hindenburg appointed him Chancellor. His aim, rather ambitiously, was to create a more broadly based government by splitting the Nazis and attracting the more socialist wing of the Nazi party, under Gregor Strasser to support him. He also hoped to gain some support from the left by a programme of public works. In this way Schleicher intended to project himself as the Chancellor of national reconciliation. However, his political manoeuvres came to nothing. The trades unions remained deeply suspicious of his motives and, encouraged by their political masters from the Social Democratic Party, broke off the negotiations. Strasser did respond to Schleicher's overtures, but Hitler retained the loyalty of the party's leadership. This left Strasser isolated and he was forced to resign. Nevertheless, the incident had been a major blow to party morale and tensions remained high in the last few weeks of 1932 as the prospect of achieving power seemed to drift away.

Hitler's fortunes did not begin to take a more favourable turn until the first week of 1933. Papen (and Hindenburg) had never forgiven Schleicher for the way he had been dropped. Papen was determined to regain political office and he now recognised that this could be achieved only by convincing President Hindenburg that he could muster majority support in the *Reichstag*. Consequently, secret contacts were made with Nazi leaders which culminated in a meeting on 4 January 1933 between Papen and Hitler. Here it was agreed in essence that Hitler should head a Nazi-Nationalist coalition government with Papen as Vice-Chancellor.

Back-stage intrigue to unseat Schleicher now took over. Papen looked for support for his plan from major landowners, leaders of industry and the army. It was only now that the conservative establishment thought that they had identified an escape from the threat of communism and the dangerous intrigues of Schleicher. Above all though, Papen had to convince the President himself. Undoubtedly encouraged by his son Oskar and his State Secretary Meissner, Hindenburg eventually gave in. Schleicher had failed in his attempt to bring stability. In fact, he had only succeeded in frightening the powerful vested interests with his ambitious plans. Hindenburg, therefore, heeded the advice of Papen to make Hitler Chancellor of a coalition government, secure in the knowledge that the Nazis would be overwhelmed by traditional conservatives and Nationalists. On 28 January 1933 Hindenburg withdrew his support for Schleicher as Chancellor; two days later he appointed Hitler to head a coalition government of 'national concentration'.

5 Why did the Nazis Replace the Weimar Republic?

From the very start, Hitler's appointment as Chancellor in January 1933 prompted extensive analysis both inside and outside Germany. This was to some extent a result of Germany's vital political and strategic position within Europe, but it was also a reflection of the interest which the 'Bohemian corporal', as Hindenburg called him, and his movement generated. Nowadays, as then, the debate about Hitler's coming to power concentrates on the historical issue of causation. In particular, it prompts two key questions, which although intimately linked, are different. 'Why did Weimar democracy fail?' and 'Why did the Nazis, and not some other political group, take power?' It is the latter question which is the real focus of this particular volume, although clearly any explanation of the Nazi take-over has to bear in mind the weaknesses and failings of the Weimar Republic: its creation out of military defeat; its association with the Treaty of Versailles; the compromise constitution; the on-going economic problems; and the political uncertainties created by short-lived coalition governments. By 1932 only 43 per cent of the electorate voted in the July *Reichstag* elections for pro-republican parties. The majority of the German people had voted in a free (and reasonably fair) election to reject democracy, despite the fact that there was no clear alternative at this time. So why was it that the Nazis assumed the mantle of power just six months later?

The Depression had transformed the Nazis into a *mass* movement. Admittedly, 63 per cent of Germans never voted for them, but 37 per cent did, so that the Nazi Party became by far the strongest party in a multi-party democracy. The Depression had led to such profound social and economic hardship that it created an environment of discontent which, in conjunction with Weimar's other failings, could easily be exploited by the Nazis' style of political activity. Indeed, it must be questionable whether Hitler would have become a national

Photomontage by John Heartfield, 1932 – 'His Majesty Adolf I lead you to magnificent disasters!'

political figure without the severity of the economic down-turn (that, of course, is not to say that the Weimar Republic would have survived in the long term). However, his mixture of racist, nationalist and anti-democratic ideas were readily received by a broad spectrum of German people, and especially by the disgruntled middle classes. There can be little doubt that Nazi ideology did successfully identify itself with certain populist fears and desires which had already found expression in the intellectual and cultural history of Germany over the previous century.

Yet, other extreme right-wing groups with similar ideas and conditions did not enjoy similar success. This is partially explained by the effective manner in which the Nazi message was communicated: the use of modern propaganda techniques; the violent exploitation of scapegoats, especially the Jews and communists; and the well-organised structure of the Party apparatus. All these factors undoubtedly helped, but in terms of electoral appeal it is impossible to ignore the powerful impact of Hitler himself as a charismatic leader with a cult following of almost messianic proportions. Furthermore, he exhibited a quite extraordinary political acumen and ruthlessness when he was involved in the *minutiae* of political in-fighting.

Nevertheless, the huge popular following of the Nazis, which so vitally undermined the continued operation of democracy, was insufficient on its own to give Hitler power. In the final analysis, it was the mutual recognition by Hitler and the representatives of the traditional leaders of the army, the landowners and heavy industry that they needed each other which led to Hitler's appointment as Chancellor of a coalition government on 30 January 1933. Ever since September 1930 every government had been forced to resort almost continuously to the use of presidential emergency decrees because they lacked a popular mandate. The only other realistic alternative to including the Nazis in the government in the chaos of 1932 was some kind of military regime – a presidential dictatorship backed by the army, perhaps. However, that too would have faced similar difficulties – indeed, by failing to satisfy the extreme left and the extreme right there would have been a very real possibility of civil war. A coalition with Hitler's Nazis therefore provided the conservative elites both with mass support and some alluring promises: a vigorous attack on Germany's political left wing; and rearmament as a precursor to economic and political expansion abroad. For Hitler, the inclusion of Papen, Hugenberg and von Blomberg gave his cabinet an air of conservative respectability. In the end, Hitler became Chancellor because the political forces of the left and centre were respectively too divided and too weak, and because the conservative right wing was prepared to accept him as a partner in government in the mistaken belief that he could be tamed. With hindsight, it can be seen that the 30 January 1933 was decisive. The dictatorship did not start technically until the completion of the 'legal

WOULD HITLER HAVE CAN TO POWER
IF THERE HADN'T BEEN ECONOMIC DOWN-TURN?

Why did the Nazis Replace the Weimar Republic? 41

revolution' in February–March 1933, but Hitler was already entrenched in power and, as one historian has claimed, now he 'could only be removed by an earthquake'.

HITLER INVITED to BE CHANCELLOR

Making notes on 'The Nazi Road to Power, 1930–3'

It is very likely that you will be asked to write an essay question using the material from this chapter. Your notes will, therefore, need to be good enough to provide you with a broad factual and analytical overview. Sections 1 and 4 are very detailed, and you should regard the finer points as an aid to understanding rather than requiring comprehensive notes. Sections 2, 3 and 5 discuss points of analysis and need to

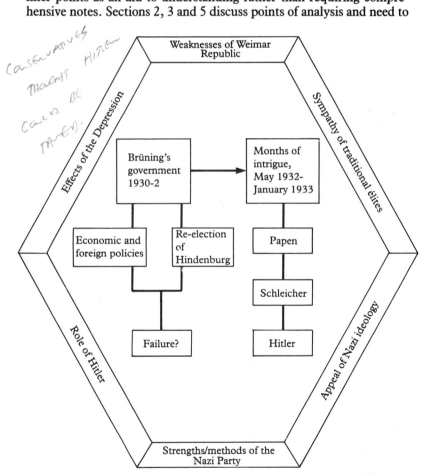

CONSERVATIVES HITLER
THOUGHT HITLER
COULD BE
TAMED.

Summary – The Nazi Road to Power

be well understood rather than memorised in detail.

The following headings, sub-headings and questions should provide a suitable framework for your notes:

1   Semi-dictatorship
1.1 Brüning's government: his aims; successes; failures.
1.2 Did Brüning fall from power because he had failed?
2   Nazi Voters
2.1 Why did the Nazis have such a broad appeal?
2.2 Why did they attract greater support from: the young; the middle classes; Protestants; the countryside?
3   Nazi Political Methods
3.1 Propaganda techniques.
3.2 Nazi use of violence.
4   The Appointment of Hitler as Chancellor
4.1 The intrigues of July 1932 to January 1933.
4.2 Assess the parts played by Schleicher, Papen and Hindenburg in the events leading to Hitler's appointment.
5   Why did the Nazis Replace the Weimar Republic?
5.1 What were the major factors which contributed to the eventual creation of the Hitler-led coalition?

Answering essay questions on 'The Nazi Road to Power, 1930–3'

Many of the questions you will be expected to answer on this topic will be variations and combinations of 'Why did the Weimar Republic fail?' and 'Why did Hitler become Chancellor of Germany?' Some examples are:

1 Why was Hitler able to come to power only 10 years after the failed Munich putsch of 1923?
2 'In the 1920s the Weimar Republic was able to resist non-democratic forces: in the 1930s it could not.' Why was this?
3 What attracted German voters to the Nazi Party between 1929 and 1933?
4 Account for the Weimar Republic's failure to resist the rise of Nazism?
5 Why did Hitler become the most powerful opponent of the Weimar Republic?

To answer such questions effectively will require a knowledge and understanding of material from both chapters 2 and 3 of this volume and also from your study of the Weimar Republic. In all these questions you are being asked to explain 'why'. You must not be tempted to write a descriptive narrative. Instead, you must use the wealth of factual material as evidence for your analysis.

A good way to tackle such explanatory questions is to draw up a list based upon a number of reasons or factors which start with the word 'because'. For example, in question 4, you could include the following:

because of the effects of the depression
because of the Nazi policy of legality
because of the Weimar Republic's basic weakness
because of Nazi propaganda

What other reasons or factors would you include?

When you have compiled a list, try to arrange the items into logical sets such as: long-term, short-term and immediate causes; or political, economic, and social factors. This will provide you with an essay plan divided into 3 or 4 organised sections – one for each set. Draw up such a plan for question 4.

In writing your essay, develop each of the sections, including the historical details, to support your argument. However, it is very important to realise that you will have to be selective in your choice of factual material. In a typical examination essay of 45 minutes you will probably have no more than 10 minutes per section! You must therefore exploit only the most relevant historical detail, bearing in mind the demands of the question and the limits of time. It is no good writing a brilliant first section if you only have 15 minutes left for the other three! Good essay planning should help you to overcome the problems of timing in the examination room.

Finally, the essay will require a conclusion. It is all too easy with an explanatory essay to use the final paragraph merely to summarise your points. This is unlikely to earn you any extra marks because you are not adding anything of importance to your answer. So, in your conclusion try to assess what you consider to be the most significant cause(s). Alternatively, show how the various factors relate to each other. This is important because a well-ordered explanatory essay can too easily appear as a series of water-tight compartments. Historical causation is normally about the inter-action of forces, and it would be a good idea for your conclusion to try to reflect this.

Source-based questions on 'The Nazi Road to Power, 1930–3'

1 Nazi Use of Propaganda

Read the extracts from *Mein Kampf* and the Propaganda Department on pages 33 and 34. Study the election poster on page 35. Answer the following questions:

a) Explain in your own words how Hitler viewed the electorate. (**4 marks**)
b) At whom is the poster directed? In what ways does the poster try to gain the support of the electorate? (**5 marks**)
c) How far does the poster reflect the attitudes expressed in the two written extracts? (**4 marks**)
d) The Nazis placed enormous importance on the role of propaganda. How significant was propaganda in creating the political success of National Socialism? (**7 marks**)

2 Hitler's Political Image
Study the photomontage on page 39. Answer the following questions:
a) Explain in your own words how the artist has portrayed Hitler. (**4 marks**)
b) What is the political message which the artist is trying to convey? (**5 marks**)
c) In what ways do you think the Nazis might have considered this photomontage rather flattering? (**6 marks**)

[handwritten: position of chancellor is dependent of president = limited]

The Nazis' Consolidation of Power, 1933–4

1 The 'Legal Revolution'

Although Hitler had been appointed Chancellor, his power was by no means absolute. Hindenburg had not been prepared to sanction Hitler's appointment until he had been satisfied that the Chancellor's power would remain limited. Such was Papen's confidence about Hitler's restricted room for manoeuvre that he boasted to a friend, 'In two months we'll have pushed Hitler into a corner so hard that he'll be squeaking'. *[handwritten: power of Hitler was greatly underestimated]*

At first sight the confidence of the conservatives seemed to be justified, since Hitler's position in purely constitutional terms was not strong. Firstly, there were only two other Nazis in the Cabinet of 12 – Wilhelm Frick as Minister of the Interior, and Hermann Göring as a minister without portfolio. Secondly, the Nazi-Nationalist coalition did not have a majority in the *Reichstag*; and thirdly, the Chancellor's post, as the previous 12 months had clearly shown, was dependent on the whim of President Hindenburg who openly resented Hitler. Yet, within two months these limitations were shown to be ineffectual, and Hitler had effectively become a dictator. Moreover, this was to be achieved by a continuation of the policy of legality which the party had pursued since 1925. How and why did this happen?

Hitler already possessed several key advantages when he became Chancellor. He was the leader of the largest political party in Germany, and it had already been shown that a policy of ignoring him did not work. During 1932 it had only led to the ineffectual governments of Papen and Schleicher. Therefore, political realism forced the conservatives to work with him. They probably needed him more than he needed them. The alternative to Hitler was civil war or a communist coup – or so it seemed to many people at the time. More importantly perhaps, the Nazi Party had now gained access to the resources of the state. For example, Göring not only had a place in the cabinet but was also Minister of the Interior in Prussia, the largest federal state, with responsibility for the police. It was a responsibility which he used blatantly to harrass opponents, while ignoring Nazi excesses. Goebbels, likewise, saw and exploited the propaganda opportunities on behalf of the Nazis. 'The struggle is a light one now,' he confided in his diary, 'since we are able to employ all the means of the State. Radio and Press are at our disposal.' Above all, however, Hitler was a masterly political tactician, and he was determined to achieve absolute power for himself. It soon became clear that Papen's political puppet was too clever to be strung along by a motley collection of ageing conservatives.

a) The *Reichstag* Election of 5 March 1933

Hitler lost no time in removing his strings. Within 24 hours of his appointment as Chancellor, new *Reichstag* elections had been called. A somewhat half-hearted attempt had been made to gain the backing of the Centre Party, but Hitler did not want any more conditions placed upon him. Anyway he felt new elections would not only increase the Nazi vote, but would enhance his own status.

The campaign for the last *Reichstag* elections held according to the Weimar constitution had few of the characteristics expected of liberal democracy: violence and terror dominated; and meetings of the Socialists and Communists were regularly broken up. In Prussia, Göring used his authority to enrol an extra 50,000 into the police – nearly all were members of the SA and SS! Altogether 69 people died during the five week campaign. However, the atmosphere of hate and fear generated by the Nazis was also used by them to great effect in their election propaganda. Hitler set the tone in his 'Appeal to the German People' of 31 January 1933. He blamed the prevailing conditions on democratic government and the terrorist activities of the Communists. He cultivated the idea of the government as a 'National Uprising' determined to restore Germany's pride and its unity. In this way he played on the inner-most desires of many Germans, but never committed himself to the details of a political and economic programme.

Hitler's 'Appeal to the German People', 31 January 1933

1 Over 14 years have passed since that unhappy day when the
German people, blinded by promises made by those at home and
abroad, forgot the highest values of our past, of the Reich, of its
honour and its freedom, and thereby lost everything. Since those
5 days of treason, the Almighty has withdrawn his blessing from
our nation. Discord and hatred have moved in. Filled with the
deepest distress, millions of the best German men and women
from all walks of life see the unity of the nation disintegrating in a
welter of egoistical political opinions, economic interests and
10 ideological conflicts . . .
   The misery of our people is terrible! The starving industrial
proletariat have become unemployed in their millions, while the
whole middle and artisan class have been made paupers. If the
German farmer also is involved in this collapse we shall be faced
15 with a catastrophe of vast proportions. For in that case, there will
collapse not only a Reich, but also a 2000-year-old inheritance of
the highest works of human culture and civilisation . . .
   It is an appalling inheritance which we are taking over. The
task before us is the most difficult which has faced German

20 statesmen in living memory. But we all have unbounded confidence, for we believe in our nation and in its eternal values.
Farmers, workers and the middle class must unite to contribute
the bricks wherewith to build the new Reich.

The National Government will therefore regard it as its first
25 and supreme task to restore to the German people unity of mind
and will. It will preserve and defend the foundations on which the
strengths of our nation rests. It will take under its firm protection
Christianity as the basis of our morality, and the family as the
nucleus of our nation and state. Standing above estates and
30 classes, it will bring back to our people the consciousness of its
racial and political unity and the obligations arising therefrom . . .
It will therefore declare merciless war on spiritual, political and
cultural nihilism. Germany must not and will not sink into
Communist anarchy.
35 In 14 years the November parties have ruined the German
farmer.

In 14 years they created an army of millions of unemployed.

The National Government will carry out the following plan
with iron resolution and dogged perseverance.
40 Within four years the German farmer must be saved from
pauperism.

Within four years unemployment must be overcome.

Parallel with this, there emerge the prerequisites for the
recovery of the economy . . .
45 The Government of the National Uprising wishes to set to
work, and it will work. It has not for 14 years brought ruin to the
German nation; it wants to lead it to the summit. It is determined
to make amends in four years for the liabilities of 14 years.

But it cannot subject the work of reconstruction to the will of
50 those who were responsible for the breakdown.

The Marxist parties and their followers had 14 years to prove
their abilities. The result is a heap of ruins.

Now, German people, give us four years and then judge us.

Let us begin, loyal to the command of the Field Marshall. May
55 Almighty God favour our work, shape our will in the right way,
bless our vision and bless us with the trust of our people. We have
no desire to fight for ourselves; only for Germany.

Another important difference in this election campaign was the
improved Nazi financial situation. Many contemporary commentators,
especially those on the left wing, portrayed Hitler as a pawn of big
business, which was said to be pouring money into the Party's coffers.
However, recent research suggests that it was not until after Hitler
became Chancellor that the big donations from commerce and industry
came flooding in. Nonetheless, at a meeting on 20 February with 20

leading industrialists, Hitler was promised 3 million Reichsmarks. With such financial backing and Goebbels' exploitation of the media, the Nazis were confident of securing a parliamentary majority.

As the election campaign moved towards its climax, one further bizarre incident strengthened the Nazi hand. On 27 February the *Reichstag* building was set on fire, and a young Dutch Communist, van der Lubbe, was arrested in incriminating circumstances. At the time it was believed by many that the entire incident was a Nazi plot to substantiate the claims of an impending Communist coup, and thereby to justify Nazi repression. However, to this day the episode has defied satisfactory explanation. A major investigation in 1962 concluded that van der Lubbe had acted alone; but 18 years later the West Berlin authorities posthumously acquitted him. It is probable that the true explanation behind the start of the fire will never now be known, although there can be little doubt about the cynical way in which the Nazis exploited the incident to their advantage.

On the next day, 28 February, Frick drew up and Hindenburg signed the 'Decree for the Protection of People and State'. In a few short clauses most civil and political liberties were suspended, and the power of central government was strengthened over state governments – all ostensibly because of the threat posed by the Communists. Following this, in the last week of the election campaign, hundreds of the Nazis' political opponents were arrested, and the violence reached new heights.

In this atmosphere of intimidation Germany went to the polls on 5 March. Somewhat surprisingly, the Nazis only increased their vote from 33.1 per cent to 43.9 per cent, thereby securing 288 seats. Hitler could only claim a majority in the new *Reichstag* with the help of the 52 seats won by the Nationalists. It was not only disappointing, it was also a political blow since any change in the existing Weimar Constitution required a two-thirds majority in the *Reichstag*.

[handwritten margin note: HAPPY HE GOT THE VOTES, BUT DIDN'T WIN A MAJORITY.]

b) The Enabling Act, March 1933

Despite this constitutional hurdle, Hitler decided to propose to the new *Reichstag* an Enabling Bill which would effectively do away with parliamentary procedure and legislation and which would instead transfer full powers to the Chancellor and his government for the next four years. In this way the dictatorship would be grounded in legality. However, the successful passage of the Enabling Bill was wholly dependent upon the support or abstention of other political parties.

A further problem was created by the fact that the momentum built up within the lower ranks of the Party during the election campaign was proving difficult for Hitler to contain. This was the so-called 'revolution from below'. It threatened to destroy Hitler's image of legality, and antagonise the conservative vested interests and his Nationalist allies.

Such was his concern that a grandiose act of reassurance was arranged. On 21 March at Potsdam Garrison Church, Goebbels orchestrated the ceremony to celebrate the opening of the *Reichstag*. In the presence of Hindenburg, the Crown Prince (the son of Kaiser Wilhelm II), and many of the army's leading generals, Hitler aligned National Socialism with the forces of the old Germany. The 'Day of Potsdam' was later described by Erich Ebermeyer:

1 A sea of flags in all the streets. We too couldn't opt out. So I get the old black-white-red gold flag from the World War down from the loft . . .
How marvellously it's been staged by that master producer
5 Goebbels. The procession of Hindenburg, the Government, and the deputies goes from Berlin to Potsdam past a solid line of cheering millions. The whole of Berlin seems to be on the streets . . . The radio announcer almost weeps with emotion.
Then Hindenburg reads his speach. Plain, strong, coming from
10 a simple heart and so presumably speaking to simple hearts . . . he now, soon to die, presides over the marriage of his world with the new rising one which the Austrian corporal, Hitler, represents. Then Hitler speaks. It cannot be denied. He has grown in stature. Out of the demagogue and party leader, the fanatic and agitator
15 . . . a true statesman seems to be developing . . . The Government's declaration is marked by notable moderation. Not a word of hatred for the opposition, not a word of racial ideology, no threat aimed at home or abroad. Hitler says only what they want: the maintenance of the great traditions of our nation, firmness of
20 government instead of eternal wavering, consideration for all the experiences of individual and human life which have proved useful for the welfare of mankind over thousands of years.
Hindenburg lays wreaths on the graves of the Prussian kings. The old Field Marshal shakes hands with the World War
25 corporal. The corporal makes a deep bow over the hand of the Field Marshal. Cannons thunder over Potsdam – over Germany.
No one can escape the emotion of the moment. Father too is deeply impressed. Mother has tears in her eyes.
In the evening a quiet hour with M. He is completely unmoved
30 by the day's events as if he was surrounded by a thick protective skin. He considers the whole thing simply a put up job, doesn't waver for one moment from his instinctive dislike. 'You've got it coming to you', says the 21 year old.
I remain silent, ashamed and torn.

Two days later the new *Reichstag* met in the Kroll Opera House to consider the Enabling Bill, and on this occasion the Nazis revealed a very different image. The Communists (those not already in prison) were refused admittance, whilst the deputies in attendance faced a barrage of intimidation from the massed ranks of the SA which surrounded the building. A Social Democrat later described the scene:

1 The wide square in front of the Kroll Opera House was crowded with dark masses of people. We were received with wild choruses: 'We want the Enabling Act!' Youths with swastikas on their chests eyed us insolently, blocked our way, in fact made us run
5 the gauntlet, calling us names like 'Centre pig', 'Marxist sow'. The Kroll Opera House was crawling with armed SA and SS men . . . The assembly hall was decorated with swastikas and similar ornaments. The diplomats' boxes and the row of seats for the audience were overcrowded. When we Social Democrats had
10 taken our seats on the extreme left, SA and SS men lined along the walls behind us in a semi-circle. Their expressions boded no good.

However, the Nazis still required a two-thirds majority to pass the bill and, on the assumption that the Social Democrats would vote against, they needed the backing of the Centre Party. Hitler thus promised in his speech of 23 March to respect the rights of the Catholic Church and to uphold religious and moral values. These were false promises, which the Centre Party deputies deceived themselves into believing. In the end only the Social Democrats voted against, and the Enabling Bill was passed by 444 to 94 votes.

Germany had succumbed to what Bracher has called 'legal revolution'. Within the space of a few weeks Hitler had legally dismantled the Weimar constitution. The way was now open for him to create a one-party totalitarian dictatorship.

2 *Gleichschaltung*

The Enabling Act was the constitutional foundation-stone of the Third Reich. In purely legal terms the Weimar constitution was never dissolved, but in practice the Enabling Act provided the basis for creating the arbitrary dictatorship which evolved in the course of 1933. The intolerance and violence exhibited by the Nazis along the road to power could now be converted into a tool of government, thus legally sanctioning the creation of a personal and party dictatorship under Hitler and the Nazis. The destruction of Weimar's remaining hallmarks of an open, liberal and pluralist society into the Nazi state system is usually referred to as *Gleichschaltung* – literally 'bringing into line' or, more commonly, 'co-ordination'. To some extent *Gleichschaltung* was generated by the power and freedom now enjoyed by the massed ranks of the SA at the local level – in effect a 'revolution from below'. But it was also directed by the Nazi leadership from the political centre in

Berlin – in effect a 'revolution from above'. Together these two political impulses attempted to 'co-ordinate' as many aspects of German life as possible along Nazi lines, although differences over the exact long-term goals of National Socialism laid the basis for future conflict within the Party.

What did *Gleichschaltung* mean in practice? It has been described rather neatly as the 'honeycombing' of German society with party associations and institutions. In other words, it was the deliberate attempt to Nazify the life of Germany. At first many of these Nazi creations had to live alongside existing bodies, but over the years they gradually superseded them. In this way much of Germany's cultural, educational and social life was increasingly controlled (see chapter 6). However, in the spring and summer of 1933 it was the 'co-ordination' of Germany's political system which was the real focus of attention, for the continued existence of the federal states, the political parties and a labour movement were totally at odds with Nazi political aspirations.

Germany had a very strong historical tradition of particularism (the devolution of political powers away from the centre to the provinces), which since unification in 1871 had found expression in the continued existence of the previously independent states as largely self-governing federal states within the unitary *Reich*. Yet, such autonomy stood in marked contrast to Nazi desires to create a fully unified country. Already Nazi activists had exploited the judicial freedom of February–March 1933 to intimidate opponents and to infiltrate federal governments. Indeed, their 'success' rapidly degenerated into violent excesses which seemed beyond the control of Hitler, who called for restraint because he was afraid of losing the support of the conservatives. Thereafter, the situation was given legal basis in April 1933 by two laws which allowed the Nazi-dominated state governments to enact legislation without reference to their *Landtage* (provincial parliaments) and which, secondly, created 18 *Reichstatthalter* (Reich governors) – often the local party *Gauleiters* – with full powers. Centralisation was taken a stage further in January 1934 when the *Landtage* were abolished and the federal governments and governors were strictly subordinated to the Ministry of the Interior. The federal principle of government was as good as dead in the Third Reich. Even the Nazi Reich governors existed only 'to execute the will of the supreme leadership of the Reich'.

Germany's trade union movement was powerful by dint of its mass membership and its strong connections with the alternative ideologies of socialism and Catholicism. Back in 1920 it had clearly revealed its industrial muscle when it had successfully ended a right-wing putsch by calling a general strike. On the whole, German organised labour was hostile to Nazism and therefore it potentially posed a major threat to the continued stability of the Nazi state. Yet, by May 1933 it was shown to be a spent force. Admittedly the Depression had already quite severely weakened it by reducing membership and lessening the will to resist, but like so many others, the trade union leaders deceived themselves into believing that they could work with the Nazis and thereby preserve a degree of independence and at least the structure of trade unionism. It was hoped that this would at least allow trade unionism to continue with its social role in the short term, while in the long term providing the framework for development in the post-Nazi era.

However, such self-deception contributed to the labour movement falling prey to a typical piece of Nazi duplicity. The Nazis surprisingly declared 1 May (the traditional day of celebration for international socialist labour) a national holiday, which gave the impression to the trade unions that perhaps there was some scope for co-operation. This proved to be the shortest of illusions. The following day, trade union premises were occupied by the SA and SS and many of the leaders were arrested. All German workers' organisations were then engulfed in DAF (*Deutscher Arbeitsfront* – German Labour Front), which acted more as an instrument of control than as a representative body of workers' interests and concerns. The power of the German trade union movement had been decisively broken. Not only was it politically emasculated, but it had even lost the most fundamental right to negotiate wages and conditions of work.

Of course, it was inconceivable that the Nazi policy of *Gleichschaltung* could allow the continued existence of other political parties. Nazism rejected democracy and any concessions to alternative opinions. Instead, it aspired to establish authoritarian rule within a one-party state. This did not prove difficult to achieve. The Communists had been proscribed since the *Reichstag* fire, and on 22 June the Social Democrats were officially banned. Yet, all the other major parties adopted a policy of 'self-*Gleichschaltung*' in the course of June and July 1933. Even the Nationalists obligingly opted for self-dissolution. Thus, there was no forum for opposition to the government decree of 14 July which formally proclaimed the Nazi Party as the only legal political party in Germany.

By the middle of 1933 the process of *Gleichschaltung* was well-advanced in many spheres of political, social and public life in Germany, although it was certainly far from complete. In particular, it had failed to make any impression on the role and influence of the Christian churches, the army and big business. This was mainly due to Hitler's determination to regulate the 'revolution from above' and to avoid antagonising such powerful vested interests. However, there were many in the lower ranks of the party who had already contributed to the 'revolution from below' and who now wanted to extend the process of *Gleichschaltung*. It was this internal party conflict which laid the basis for the bloody events of June 1934.

3 The Night of the Long Knives

In a speech on 6 July 1933 to the Reich governors, Hitler warned of the dangers posed by a permanent state of revolution. He therefore formally declared an end to the revolution and demanded that 'the stream of revolution must be guided into the safe channel of evolution'. He was increasingly concerned that the behaviour of party activists was running beyond his control and that it was likely to create political embarrassment in his relations with the conservative forces upon whose support he still depended. His speech amounted to a clear and unequivocal demand that the party accept not only the realities of political compromise, but also the necessity of change from above and not from below.

Hitler's appeal failed to have the desired effect. If anything, it substantiated the fears of many ordinary Nazis that the leadership was prepared to dilute the radical ideology of National Socialism for reasons of political expediency. Such concerns gave rise to demands for the implementation of a second, more radical revolution, which would not hold back from attacking the forces of the German establishment. These calls for further revolutionary action came most strongly from within the ranks of the SA.

The SA tended to represent the populist, anti-capitalist, left wing of the Nazi Party, which to a large extent reflected its more working-class membership. It placed far more emphasis on the socialist elements of the Party programme than Hitler ever did and therefore saw no need to hold back simply for the sake of satisfying conservative social forces. It had played a vital role in the years of struggle by winning the political battle in the streets, and many of its members were embittered by the compromises being made by the regime. They were also disappointed by the limited personal benefits that were accruing from the acquisition of power. Such views were epitomised by the leader of the SA, Ernst Röhm, who called for a genuine 'National Socialist Revolution' and who was increasingly disillusioned by the politics of his old friend Hitler. However, at the very heart of the developing confrontation lay the future role of the SA in the Nazi state. Röhm had no desire to see the SA degenerate into a mere propaganda appendage now that the street-fighting was over. He wanted to integrate the army and the SA into a people's militia of which he would be the commander. In a private interview in early 1934 with a local Party boss, Röhm gave vent to his feelings and his ideas:

1 Adolf is a swine. He will give us all away. He only associates with
   the reactionaries now . . . Getting matey with the East Prussian
   generals. They're his cronies now . . . Adolf knows exactly what I
   want. I've told him often enough. Not a second edition of the old
5 imperial army. Are we revolutionaries or aren't we? . . . If we are,

then something new must arise out of our *elan*, like the mass
armies of the French Revolution. If we're not then we'll go to the
dogs. We've got to produce something new, don't you see? A new
discipline of organisation. The generals are a lot of old fogeys.
10 They never had a new idea . . . I'm the nucleus of the new army,
don't you see that? Don't you understand that what's coming
must be new, fresh and unused? The basis must be revolutionary.
You can't inflate it afterwards. You only get the opportunity once
to make something new and big that'll help us lift the world off its
15 hinges. But Hitler puts me off with fair words.

Such a plan was anathema to the army who saw their traditional role
and status being directly threatened. Hitler was caught in an unenviable
position between two powerful but rival forces, either of which could
create considerable political difficulties for him. On the one hand, the
SA consisted of two and a half million committed Nazis and was led by
his oldest political friend. On the other hand, the army was the one
organisation which could unseat him from his position of power.
Moreover, it alone possessed the military skills which were vital to the
success of his foreign policy aims; however large the SA was, it could
never hope to challenge the discipline, fighting spirit and professional
expertise possessed by the army.

Political realities dictated that Hitler had to maintain the backing of
the army, but in the winter of 1933–4 he was still loath to engineer a
show-down with his old friend, Röhm. He tried to appease Röhm by
bringing him into the cabinet. He also called a meeting in February
between the leaders of the army, the SA and the SS in an attempt to
reach an agreement about the role of each organisation within the Nazi
state. However, the tension did not subside. Röhm and the SA resented
Hitler's apparent acceptance of the privileged position of the army,
while their own unrestrained actions and ill-discipline only increased
the feelings of dissatisfaction amongst the generals.

The developing crisis came to a head in the spring of 1934 when it
became apparent that President Hindenburg did not have much longer
to live. The political implications of his imminent death were profound.
Hitler clearly wanted to assume the presidency without opposition. He
certainly did not want a contested election, nor did he have any
sympathy for those conservatives who desired the restoration of the
monarchy. It was the necessity of securing the army's unqualified
backing for his succession to Hindenburg which seems to have forced
Hitler's hand. The support of the army had become the key to his
regime's survival in the short term, while in the long term it offered the
means to fulfilling his ambitions in the field of foreign affairs. Whatever
personal loyalty Hitler felt for Röhm and the SA was now finally put to
one side. The army desired their elimination and an end to all the talk
of 'a second revolution' and 'a people's militia'. By agreeing to this,

Hitler could gain the favour of the army generals, secure his personal position and remove an increasingly embarrassing mill-stone from around his neck. Although written evidence of an agreement between Hitler and the army generals does not exist, it is known that the two parties did meet on the battleship *Deutschland* in April 1934. Also an analysis of the actual events of June 1934 strongly suggests that there was a clear mutual understanding directed against the SA. Furthermore, influential voices within the Nazi Party, in particular Göring and Himmler, were also manoeuvring behind the scenes towards a similar goal in order to further their own ambitions by decisively weakening a powerful rival.

On 30 June 1934, the 'Night of the Long Knives', Hitler eliminated the SA as a political and military force once and for all. Röhm and the main leaders of the SA were shot by members of the SS – although the weapons and transport were provided by the army. There was no resistance of any substance. In addition, various old scores were settled: Schleicher, the former Chancellor, and Strasser, the leader of the socialist/anti-capitalist wing of the Nazi Party, were both killed. Altogether it is estimated that 400 people were murdered. On 5 July the *Völkischer Beobachter* newspaper reported on the Reich cabinet meeting held two days earlier:

1 ... The Reich Chancellor began by giving a detailed account of the origin and suppression of the high treason plot. The Reich Chancellor stressed that lightning action had been necessary, otherwise many thousands of people would have been in danger
5 of being wiped out.

Defence Minister General von Blomberg thanked the Führer in the name of the Reich Cabinet and the army for his determined and courageous action, by which he had saved the German people from civil war. The Führer had shown greatness as a statesman
10 and a soldier. This had aroused in the hearts of the members of the cabinet and of the whole German people a vow of service, devotion and loyalty in this grave hour.

The Reich Cabinet then approved a law on measures for the self-defence of the State. Its single paragraph reads: 'The mea-
15 sures taken on 30 June and 1 and 2 July to suppress the acts of high treason are legal, being necessary for the self-defence of the State.'

It would be difficult to overestimate the significance of the Night of the Long Knives. The army had unequivocally aligned itself behind the Nazi regime, as was shown by Blomberg's public vote of thanks to Hitler on 1 July, while the SA was reduced to the role of a propaganda show-piece and thereafter played no significant role in the political development of the Nazi state. More ominously for the future, it marked the emergence of the SS as the Party's elite institution of terror. Above all, Hitler had secured his own personal political supremacy. On 13 July 1934 he told the *Reichstag*:

1 If disaster was to be prevented at all, action must be taken with lightning speed. Only a ruthless and bloody intervention might still perhaps stifle the spread of the revolt . . . If anyone reproaches me and asks why I did not resort to the regular courts of
5 justice for conviction of the offenders, then all that I can say to him is this: in this hour I was responsible for the fate of the German people, and thereby I became the supreme judge of the German people.

Consequently, when Hindenburg died on 1 August, Hitler was able to merge the offices of Chancellor and President, and also to take on the new official title of Führer. The Nazi regime had been stabilised and the threat of a 'second revolution' had been completely removed.

[handwritten margin note: NEEDED SUPPORT OF CG THE PARTY]

4 The Third Reich – A Political Revolution?

At the Nuremberg party rally of September 1934 Hitler declared triumphantly and with exultant optimism:

Just as the world cannot live on wars, so people cannot live on revolutions . . . Revolutions have always been rare in Germany . . . In the next thousand years there will be no other revolution in Germany.

The word 'revolution' has figured prominently throughout this chapter. Hitler spoke of a 'national revolution', whilst Röhm demanded a 'second revolution'. Likewise, political and historical analysts have written of 'the legal revolution' and the 'revolution from below'. How appropriate is such terminology to describe the events of 1933–4? To what extent had Germany undergone a political revolution by the end of 1934?

First of all it is important to recognise that the use of the term 'revolution' is not a prerogative of the political left. It simply means a fundamental change – an overturning of existing conditions. Secondly, it is a dynamic word beloved of politicians and propagandists who use it to stir emotions and to emphasise change. All too often it is used for effect and with scant regard for its real meaning. If Germany did undergo a 'political revolution' in the course of 1933–4, the evidence must indicate that there was a decisive break in the country's line of political development.

At first sight the regime created by the Nazis by the end of 1934 seems to be the very antithesis of Germany's immediate political past.

The institutions and values of an open and pluralistic liberal democracy had been rejected and replaced by an arbitrary dictatorship. However, it should be remembered that the Weimar Republic had ceased to function as an effective democracy well before Hitler became Chancellor. Moreover, the strength of the anti-democratic forces had tormented the young democracy from the very start, so that it was never able to establish strong roots. Yet, even by comparison with pre-1918 Germany, the Nazi regime had wrought fundamental changes: the destruction of the autonomy of the federal states; the intolerance shown towards the existence of any kind of political opposition; the reduction of the *Reichstag* to complete impotence. In all these ways the process of *Gleichschaltung* decisively affected political traditions which had prevailed since the foundation of the *Kaiserreich* in 1871. In this sense it is not unfair to view the events of 1933–4 as a 'political revolution', since the Nazis had turned their backs quite categorically on the federal, liberal and constitutional values which had permeated even in an authoritarian regime like that of the *Kaiserreich*.

However, support for the idea of a Nazi political revolution must be tempered by recognising important lines of historical continuity. At the time of Hindenburg's death, major forces within Germany continued to exert an existence independent of the Nazi regime. In particular, there were the army, big business and the civil service. One might even include the Christian churches, although they did not carry the same degree of political weight. It was Hitler's willingness to enter into political partnership with these representatives of the old Germany which had encouraged Röhm and the SA to demand a 'second revolution'. The elimination of the SA in the Night of the Long Knives suggests that Hitler's 'national revolution' had just been an attractive anti-Marxist and anti-democratic slogan. In reality this 'revolution' was strictly limited in scope; it involved political compromise and it had refrained from fundamental social and economic change. In this sense one could view the early years of the Nazi regime as merely another political manifestation (albeit the most unpleasant one) of the socio-economic forces which had dominated Germany's political development since 1871.

Certainly, such an interpretation would seem to be a fair assessment of the situation up until late 1934. However, the true revolutionary extent of the regime can only be fully assessed by considering the political, social and economic developments that took place in Germany throughout the entire period of the Third Reich. These will be the *foci* of the next two chapters.

Making notes on 'The Nazis' Consolidation of Power, 1933–4'

Because this chapter discusses events that are an integral part of the
Nazis' establishment of complete political control within Germany, it is
important that you think about its contents in the context of the issues
covered in chapter 3. Therefore, it might be helpful to re-read the notes
you made on that chapter before you write anything about the events of
1933–4.

As you make your notes on this chapter try to avoid the temptation
merely to record what happened. With each event make some assessment of the part it played in the Nazis' progress towards political
dominance.

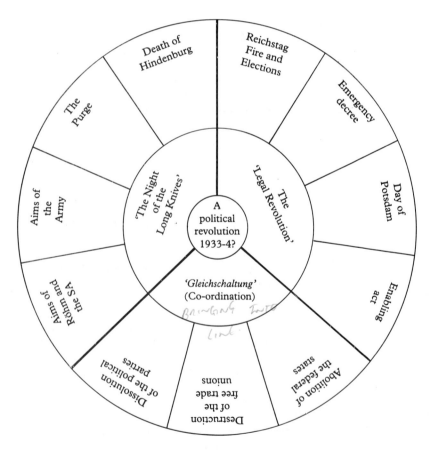

Summary – The Nazis' Consolidation of Power, 1933–4

The following headings, sub-headings and questions should assist you to structure your notes effectively:

1 The Legal Revolution

1.1 What were the strengths and weaknesses of Hitler's position in January 1933?

1.2 The *Reichstag* Fire and elections.

1.3 How did the Day of Potsdam seek to reassure?

1.4 The Enabling Act.

Having made notes on this section, do you think Bracher was right to describe the above events as a 'legal revolution'?

2 *Gleichschaltung*

As you look at the three examples make certain you understand how and why each institution could have posed a threat to the Nazis.

2.1 Federal states.

2.2 Trade unions.

2.3 Political parties.

3 The Night of the Long Knives

3.1 What is meant by the terms 'revolution from below', 'revolution from above', and 'a second revolution'?

3.2 What were the aims of the SA and the army?

3.3 When and why did Hitler decide to crush the SA?

3.4 Why is the Night of the Long Knives considered to be so significant?

4 A political revolution?

4.1 Arguments for and against.

Source-based questions on 'The Nazis' Consolidation of Power, 1933–4'

1 Hitler's 'Appeal to the German People'

Carefully read the extract 'Hitler's Appeal to the German People' on pages 46–47. Answer the following questions:

a) Explain
  i) 'the November parties' (line 35)
  ii) 'loyal to the command of the Field Marshall' (line 54). (**4 marks**)

b) To whom does Hitler appeal for moral backing for the Nazi regime? (**2 marks**)

c) In what ways does Hitler try to cultivate an image of reasonableness? (**4 marks**)

d) What rhetorical techniques does Hitler use to make his points more forcefully? (**4 marks**)

e) How far would you agree that Hitler's appeal was 'more an attack on the political opposition than a genuine political programme'? (**6 marks**)

2 Nazi Political Methods

Carefully read the extracts describing the Day of Potsdam and the passing of the Enabling Bill on pages 49 and 50. Answer the following questions:

a) Explain
   i) 'Centre pig' (page 50 line 5)
   ii) 'the demagogue' (page 49 line 14). (**2 marks**)
b) Why was Potsdam chosen for the ceremony of 21 March 1933? (**2 marks**)
c) The description of the scene at the Kroll Opera House was written by an avowed opponent of the Nazi regime. In what ways does this affect the value of the evidence to the historian? (**4 marks**)
d) What evidence is there in Ebermeyer's description to suggest that he is essentially unsympathetic to the Nazis? (**4 marks**)
e) In what ways does Ebermeyer seem to have been won over by the 'Day of Potsdam'? (**3 marks**)
f) The 'Day of Potsdam' and the passage of the Enabling Bill took place within two days of each other. How do you explain the contrast in the ways the Nazis acted on the two occasions? (**5 marks**)

3 The Night of the Long Knives

Carefully read the three extracts on the Night of the Long Knives given on pages 53, 55 and 56. Answer the following questions:

a) How did Hitler try to justify the purge to the cabinet and to the *Reichstag*? (**4 marks**)
b) From your wider knowledge of Germany in 1934, how much truth do you think there was in Röhm's claim that Hitler 'only associates with the reactionaries now'? (**4 marks**)
c) What is the significance of the law approved on 3 July? (**4 marks**)
d) What are the weaknesses of the account of the Party boss as evidence of Röhm's attitude in 1934? (**3 marks**)
e) Using the evidence from these three extracts, explain why the Night of the Long Knives is considered to be such an important turning-point. (**5 marks**)

CHAPTER 5

Politics and Economics in the Nazi State, 1933–45

1 The Concept of Totalitarianism

In his futuristic novel *Nineteen Eighty-Four* George Orwell portrayed a political system and a society which has subsequently become a 'model' of totalitarianism. There was no place for the individual in *Nineteen Eighty-Four*; every aspect of life was controlled by the party, which in turn was dominated by the all pervasive personality of 'Big Brother'. Such was the extent of this totalitarian control that telescreens in every room observed one's actions, whilst the thought police tracked down anyone whose beliefs were incompatible with party ideology. In such fictional ways Orwell took the concept of totalitarianism to its logical and absurd conclusion.

Orwell was writing in the late 1940s and his vision of totalitarianism had been stimulated to a large extent by his observations of the dictatorial regimes of the period, especially Stalin's (which is a very good reason why you, as a student of twentieth-century history, should try to read Orwell's book). However, in the 1950s a number of historians and political scientists also began to interpret the Nazi regime as an example of the totalitarian model. According to such interpretations there were no fundamental differences between the regimes of Fascist Italy, Nazi Germany and Soviet Russia. Indeed, Carl Friedrich's analysis went so far as to identify six major features common to totalitarian dictatorships: an official ideology, a single mass party, terroristic control by the police, monopolistic control over the media, a monopoly of arms, and central control of the economy – all of which he claimed existed in Mussolini's Italy, Hitler's Germany and Stalin's Russia.

Although the idea of Nazism as a form of totalitarianism held great sway in the 1950s, such a view is not now so readily accepted. However, you will often still see the term used to describe Hitler's regime. This chapter therefore examines the *balance* of forces and interest groups in the political and economic life of the Third Reich. As you read it, you should bear in mind the concept of totalitarianism and assess whether the power structure which emerges can be equated with it.

2 The Nazi System of Government

a) The Relationship between Party and State

By July 1933 Germany had become a one-party state, in which the Nazi

Party claimed sole political authority in every aspect of German life. Such totalitarian claims, augmented by a powerful propaganda machine, deceived many contemporaries into thinking that the Nazi state was a clear and well-ordered system of government. The reality was very different. Fundamentally, this was because the exact relationship between the structure and role of the Party on the one hand and the apparatus of the German state on the other was never to be clarified satisfactorily.

From the start, the existence of parallel Party and state machinery laid the basis for much of the confusion. Some of the Nazi leaders were keen to establish the Party's control over the civil and diplomatic services. This to some extent reflected the wishes of the revolutionary elements within the Party, which wanted to smash such traditional elements of government in order to create a new kind of Germany – although it also conveniently provided an avenue for self-advancement. However, others recognised that the bureaucracy of the German state was well-established and staffed by an educated personnel, which could not simply be disregarded. Initially, therefore, there was no drastic purge of the state apparatus. The *Law for the Restoration of the Professional Civil Service* of April 1933 was strictly limited in its scope. It only provided for the removal of Jews and known opponents of the regime.

Hitler himself also remained ambivalent on the issue, despite attempts from both sides to seek clarification. The *Law to ensure the Unity of Party and State* promulgated in December 1933, proclaimed that the Party 'is inseparably linked with the state', but the explanation was phrased in such nebulous terms as to be meaningless. Two months later, Hitler declared that the Party's principal responsibilities were to implement government measures and to organise propaganda and indoctrination. Yet, in September 1934 he told the Party Congress that 'it is not the state which commands us but rather we who command the state', and a year later he specifically declared that the Party would assume responsibility for those tasks which the state failed to fulfil.

Hitler's ambiguity on this issue is partially explained by the political ferment of these years and by the need to placate numerous interest groups. However, the problem was also rooted in the background and composition of the Party itself. The Party organisation had been created and had evolved as a means to *gain* political power. It had proved remarkably well designed for this purpose, but it was not geared to the task of government. Moreover, the Party itself was by no means a unified whole. It consisted of a mass of specialist organisations – such as the Hitler Youth, the German Labour Front and the NS Teachers' League. Such groups had evolved because of the need to attract support from different sections of society in the years before 1933. Once in power, such groups were keen to uphold their own particular interests – the Party had become splintered and lacked a unifying structure.

LINE RUSSIA (Lenin)

Another problem emerged in the course of 1933. As the Nazi regime established itself there took place a vast increase in Party membership as people jumped on the bandwagon of opportunity. Inevitably, this tended to dilute the influence of the old guard, thus further weakening the radical cutting edge of the Party apparatus within the regime.

However, the position of the Party did improve somewhat from the mid-1930s when Rudolf Hess, as Deputy *Führer*, was granted special powers. In 1935 he was given the right to vet the appointment and promotion of all civil servants, and to oversee the drafting of all legislation. By 1939 it had become compulsory for all civil servants to be Party members. In this way, the foundations were laid for Party supervision, if not outright domination, of the state apparatus.

The other key figure in the changing fortunes of the Party was Martin Bormann, who was a skilled and hard-working administrator with great personal ambition. Working alongside Hess, he correctly analysed the problems confronting the Party and created two new departments with the deliberate aim of strengthening the Party's position (and thereby his own). These were the Department for Internal Party Affairs, which had the task of exerting discipline within the Party structure, and the Department for Affairs of State, which aimed to secure Party supremacy over the state. Considerable success was achieved by these two departments in subsequent years, especially after 1941 when Hess's flight to England further strengthened Bormann's personal position. Thereafter, by constant meddling, by sheer perseverance and by maintaining good personal relations with Hitler, Bormann effectively advanced the Party's fortunes. By 1943, when he became Hitler's Secretary and thus secured direct access to the *Führer*, Bormann had constructed an immensely strong power-base for himself

Under Bormann's influence the Party was moulded into an institution of government rather than merely of opposition. It also succeeded in strengthening its position in respect of the traditional apparatus of the state. Undoubtedly, therefore, it was one of the key power blocs within Nazi Germany, and its influence continued to be felt until the very end. However, it must be remembered that the Party had to compete strenuously for influence with the state institutions, and the latter were never emasculated, even if they were circumscribed. Above all though, the internal divisions and rivalries within the Party itself were never entirely overcome and consequently the Nazi Party never became such an all-pervasive dominating instrument as the Bolsheviks were in Soviet Russia.

b) The Role of Hitler

What exactly was the role of Hitler himself in the political labyrinth of the Third Reich? In theory his power was unlimited. Nazi Germany was a one-party state and Hitler was undisputed leader of that Party. In addition, after the death of Hindenburg in August 1934, the *Law concerning the Head of State of the German Reich* combined the posts of President and Chancellor. Constitutionally, Hitler was also Commander-in-Chief of all the armed services.

However, if one studies contemporary constitutional documents, such as the following extract from a leading Nazi theorist, it is clear that Hitler's personal dictatorship was portrayed in more than purely legal terms:

 1 The office of *Führer* has developed out of the National Socialist
   movement. In its origins it is not a state office. The office of
   Führer has grown out of the movement into the Reich . . . The
   position of *Führer* combines in itself all sovereign power of the
 5 Reich: all public power in the state as in the movement is derived
   from the *Führer's* power. If we wish to define political power in
   the *völkisch Reich* correctly, we must not speak of 'state power'
   but of '*Führer* power'. For it is not the state as an impersonal
   entity which is the source of political power, but rather political
 10 power is given to the *Führer* as the executor of the nation's
   common will. '*Führer* power' is comprehensive and total: it unites
   within itself all means of creative political activity: it embraces all
   spheres of national life.

Such grandiose theoretical claims for '*Führer* power' could not mask basic practical problems. Firstly, there was (and is) no way one individual could ever be in control of all aspects of government. Thus Hitler was still dependent upon sympathetic subordinates to put policy decisions into effect (just as the mere passage of an Act of Parliament in Britain will never guarantee to solve a problem unless the apparatus for effective implementation exists). Additionally, Hitler's own personality and attitude towards administration were not conducive to strong and effective leadership of government. At first this may seem rather contrary to the idea of Hitler as the charismatic and dynamic leader. However, this was an image perpetuated by the propaganda machine, which really only holds any degree of validity for the years before 1933. Once in government Hitler's character revealed itself, as is shown in the post-war memoirs of one of his retinue:

 1 Hitler normally appeared shortly before lunch . . . When Hitler
   stayed at Obersalzberg it was even worse. There he never left his
   room before 2.00pm. He spent most afternoons taking a walk, in
   the evening straight after dinner, there were films . . . He disliked
 5 the study of documents. I have sometimes secured decisions from
   him without his ever asking to see the relevant files. He took the
   view that many things sorted themselves out on their own if one
   did not interfere . . . He let people tell him the things he wanted

to hear, everything else he rejected. One still sometimes hears the
10 view that Hitler would have done the right thing if people
surrounding him had not kept him wrongly informed. Hitler
refused to let himself be informed . . . How can one tell someone
the truth who immediately gets angry when the facts do not suit
him.

Hitler believed that mere will-power was the solution to most
problems. He loathed the paper-work of governmental administration
and he disliked the formality of committees in which issues could be
discussed. He was not even very decisive, when it came to making a
choice. Thus, although Hitler was portrayed as the all-powerful
dictator, he never showed any inclination to co-ordinate government.
The situation was exacerbated further by his lifestyle: the unusual
sleeping hours; the long periods of absence from Berlin; and the
tendency to become immersed in pet projects such as architectural
plans. In this way Hitler's personal behaviour as dictator directly
contributed to the chaotic government structure of Nazi Germany.

Historians are now generally in agreement about the confusion in
Nazi government. However, there remain two very distinct schools of
thought about how this should be interpreted. The so-called 'intentionalist' approach continues to uphold the absolutely vital role of
Hitler in the development of the Third Reich. Consequently, the
prevailing chaos is seen as a result of a deliberate policy of divide and
rule on the part of Hitler – in effect an attempt (and obviously
successful) to maintain his own political authority by encouraging
division and confusion in both the structure and personnel of government. This in essence, is the view to be found in the writings of
Hildebrand and Bracher. The alternative interpretation has been
dubbed 'structuralist' or 'functionalist', and is expressed most forcefully in the works of Broszat and Mommsen. They believe that the Nazi
regime and its policies evolved from the pressure of circumstances and
that the confusion in government was a true reflection of Hitler's
limitations because of the continued influence of other sources of
power. Indeed, Broszat even goes as far as to describe Hitler as
'unwilling to take decisions, frequently uncertain, exclusively concerned with upholding his prestige and personal authority, influenced
in the strongest fashion by his current entourage, in some respects a
weak dictator'.

c) The Apparatus of the Police State

Amidst all the confusion of the state and party structure there emerged
in the SS an organisation which was to become the mainstay of the
Third Reich. The SS developed an identity and structure of its own
which kept it separate from the state and yet, through its dominance of
police matters, linked it with the state.

The SS had been formed in 1925 as an elite body-guard for Hitler, but it remained a relatively minor section of the SA until Himmler became its leader in 1929. By 1933 the SS numbered 52,000, and it had established a reputation for blind obedience and total commitment to the Nazi cause. Himmler had also created in 1931 a special security service, *Sicherheitsdienst* (SD), to act as the Party's own internal police force. In the course of 1933–4 he assumed control of all the political police in the *Länder*, including the Gestapo in Prussia. Thus, Hitler turned to Himmler's SS to carry out the purge of June 1934. The loyalty and brutal efficiency of the SS on the Night of the Long Knives had its rewards, for it now became an independent organisation within the Party. Two years later all police powers were unified under Himmler's control as 'Chief of the German Police'.

As *Reichsführer* SS, Himmler controlled a massive police apparatus which was answerable only to Hitler himself. In the years to come the SS-Police-SD system grew into one of the key power blocs in the Third Reich. It assumed responsibility for all security matters; the concentration camps were run by its Death Head Units; it formed its own military divisions, which were to develop into the elite fighting units of the *Waffen SS*; and increasingly it became involved in the various racial issues.

By 1939 the SS-Police-SD system was more than 'a state within a state'. It was a huge vested interest, which had begun to eclipse other interest groups in terms of power and influence. With the onset of war this tendency was accentuated further. As German troops gained control over more and more areas of Europe, the power of the SS was inevitably enhanced. The job of internal security became much greater – by 1945 the Gestapo alone had grown to 40,000, and SS officers were granted draconian powers to crush opposition. The *Waffen* SS increased from three divisions in 1939 to 35 in 1945, so that it rivalled the power of the army. Above all, the SS became responsible for the creation of the 'New Order' in eastern Europe (the resettlement and extermination of the various 'inferior' races). Such a scheme provided opportunities for plunder and power on a massive scale, which members of the SS exploited to the full. By the end of the war the SS had created a massive commercial combine of over 150 firms, which exploited slave labour to extract raw materials and to manufacture textiles, armaments and household goods.

The SS-Police-SD system under Himmler not only preserved the Nazi regime by its brutal and repressive policies of law enforcement, but gradually extended its influence into the vital areas of military and economic affairs. In this way it became the key interest group in the Third Reich.

'Hitler's State' by Magnus Zeller

d) The Nazi Propaganda Machine

Despite the immense power of the Nazi police apparatus, it would be simplistic to believe that the regime maintained itself in power simply by the use of brutal repression. From the moment Hitler became Chancellor, propaganda played a key part in welding together the political attitudes of the nation. As Goebbels, the new Minister of Popular Enlightenment and Propaganda, stated at his first press conference on 15 March 1933:

> 1 I view the first task of the new ministry as being to establish
> co-ordination between the Government and the whole people . . .
> It is not enough for people to be more or less reconciled to our
> regime, to be persuaded to adopt a neutral attitude towards us,
> 5 rather we want to work on people until they have capitulated to
> us, until they grasp ideologically that what is happening in
> Germany today is not an end in itself, but a means to an end. If
> the means achieves the end, the means is good. Whether it always
> satisfies stringent aesthetic criteria or not is immaterial.

Such conviction, combined with the undoubted intelligence of Goebbels, made the Propaganda Ministry a vital cog in the Nazi machine, although the man himself never gained the political pre-eminence of Göring, of Himmler, and (latterly) of Bormann.

The two most important forms of media were the radio and the press. Goebbels (and Hitler) had always recognised the effectiveness of the spoken word over the written, and they had already begun to use the new technology during the election campaigns of 1932–3. Once in power, Goebbels efficiently brought all German broadcasting, which up until this time had been organized by the *Länder*, under Nazi control by the creation of the Reich Radio Company. Furthermore, he arranged the dismissal of 13 per cent of the staff on political and racial grounds, and their replacement by his own men. He told his broadcasters in March 1933:

> 1 We make no bones about the fact that the radio belongs to us and
> no one else. And we will place the radio in the service of our
> ideology and no other ideology will find expression here . . . I am
> placing a major responsibility in your hands, for you have in your
> 5 hands the most modern instrument in existence for influencing
> the masses. By this instrument you are the creators of public
> opinion.

Yet, control of broadcasting was of little value in terms of propaganda unless the people had the means to receive it, and in 1932 less than 25 per cent of German households owned a wireless. Consequently, the government made provision for the production of a cheap set, the *Volksempfänger* (People's Receiver). By 1939 70 per cent of German homes had access to a radio – the highest national figure in the world – and it became a medium of mass communication.

Broadcasting was also directed at public places. By means of loudspeakers, restaurants and cafes, factories and offices, all became channels for collective listening. 'Radio wardens' were even appointed, whose duty it was to co-ordinate the listening process.

Control of the press was not so easily achieved by Goebbels. Germany had over 4,700 daily newspapers in 1933 – a consequence of the strong regional identities which still existed in a relatively new nation state. Moreover, the papers were all owned privately, and traditionally owed no allegiance to central or local government; their loyalty was to their publishing company, religious denomination or political party. Various measures were taken to achieve Nazi control. Firstly, the Nazi publishing house, *Eher Verlag*, bought up numerous newspapers, so that by 1939 it controlled two-thirds of the German press. Secondly, the various news agencies were merged into one, the DNB; this was state controlled, with the result that news material was vetted even before it got to the journalists. Thirdly, Goebbels introduced a daily press conference at the Propaganda Ministry to provide guidance on editorial policy. And finally, by the so-called *Editors Law* of October 1933, newspaper content was made the sole responsibility of the editor; it became his job to satisfy the requirements of the Propaganda Ministry, or face the appropriate consequences. In this way, as one historian has explained, 'There was no need for censorship because the editor's most important function was that of censor'.

The Nazis certainly succeeded to a large extent in muzzling the press. Even the internationally renowned *Frankfurter Zeitung* eventually succumbed to closure in 1943. However, the price of that success was the evolution of a bland and sterile journalism, which undoubtedly contributed to the 10 per cent decline in newspaper circulation in the years 1933–9.

Although control of the press and radio was Goebbels' major objective, he gradually extended his influence so that film, music, literature and art all came under the control of the Reich Chamber of Culture. Their role will be looked at in detail in the next chapter. For the moment suffice it to say that attempts to propagate a distinctive Nazi culture were relatively unsuccessful.

One final aspect of the Goebbels propaganda machine was the deliberate attempt to create a new kind of social ritual. The *Heil Hitler* greeting, the Nazi salute, the *Horst Wessel* song and the preponderance of militaristic uniforms were all intended to strengthen the individual's identity with the regime. This was further encouraged by the establishment of a series of public festivals to commemorate historic days in the Nazi calendar.

Historic Days in the Nazi Calendar

30 January	The seizure of power (1933)
24 February	The refounding of the Party (1925)
1st Sunday in March	Heroes Remembrance Day (War Dead)
20 April	Hitler's birthday
1 May	National Day of Labour
2nd Sunday in May	Mothering Sunday
September	Nuremburg Party rally
9 November	The Munich *putsch* (1923)

It is impossible to assess how effective Nazi propaganda was in any quantitative sense. Genuine opinion polls of public attitudes were not a feature of Nazi Germany, although the Party was so concerned about public morale that it used to conduct its own surveys. However, it is perhaps rather too easy, from the standpoint of our open liberal democracy and with the advantages of hindsight, to dismiss its impact or to sneer at the gullibility of those who were taken in. To have lived in a society where only one point of view was disseminated must have blunted one's powers of judgement. When that society was also terrorised by a repressive police system and administered by an extensive Party apparatus, it was perhaps easier to believe the propaganda than to question it.   *PEOPLE   JUST HAD to GO ALONG*
WITH PROPOGANDA.

3 The Army

In any political system the role of the armed forces is vital for political stability. A regime which fails to maintain the support of the military will lack credibility in both its domestic and foreign policies. Indeed, whenever there is news of a political coup, it is usually the stance adopted by the military which proves to be the decisive factor in the survival or overthrow of the government.

In Germany the military tradition went back a long way into the nation's past. Above all, it was the reputation established by Prussian militarism which so often evoked comment. 'Prussia is not a country with an army: it is an army with a country', the French statesman Mirabeau had observed in the late eighteenth century. It was the power of the Prussian military machine which had enabled Bismarck to forge German unification out of the wars with Denmark (1864), Austria (1866) and France (1870–1). Thereafter, the army was always to be found at the centre of German political life. The military elite enjoyed great social status and the leading generals exerted considerable influence, as was shown in the intrigue of 1932–3 and in the manoeuvrings which culminated in the Night of the Long Knives. How then did the army fit into the power structure of the Third Reich? How did

Nazism, with its revolutionary and totalitarian claims, cope with such a powerful and traditional vested interest?

In the immediate aftermath of the Night of the Long Knives, it seemed as if the army was in a position of considerable strength. Unlike other institutions, it had not been 'co-ordinated' and its leaders were confident that they had gained a certain primacy as Hitler had agreed to the destruction of his own SA. Ironically, it was even believed by many army officers that the extremist element within Nazism had been removed and that they could now make the Nazi state work according to their interests and wishes. However, with hindsight, it is clear that although the army had succeeded in preserving its influence in the short term, this had been achieved by a compromise which was to be fatal in the long term. This is most clearly shown by the new oath of loyalty demanded by Hitler of all soldiers, and accepted by Field Marshal von Blomberg, the War Minister, and General von Fritsch, the Commander-in-Chief of the army.

1 I swear by God this sacred oath: that I will render unconditional obedience to the *Führer* of the German Reich and people, Adolf Hitler, the Supreme Commander of the Armed Forces, and will be ready as a brave soldier to risk my life at any time for this oath.

For a German soldier, bound by discipline and obedience such words marked a commitment which made any future resistance an act of the most serious treachery.

In the years 1934–7 the relationship between the Nazi state and the army remained cordial. Encouraged by the rearmament programme and the re-introduction of conscription in March 1935 (thereby increasing the size of the army to 550,000), the High Command deceived itself into believing that its pre-eminent position was being preserved. In fact, the power of the SS was growing fast, whilst Hitler himself had little respect for the conservative attitudes held by many officers. It was merely political realism which held him back from involvement in army affairs until 1938.

In November 1937 Hitler had outlined at the Hossbach meeting (see page 124) his foreign policy aims of expansion. Blomberg and Fritsch, given Germany's state of military unpreparedness, were both seriously concerned by Hitler's talk of war and conquest. Their doubts only served further to convince Hitler of the spineless nature of the army leadership, and in February 1938 both men were forced from office after revelations about their private lives. Blomberg had just married for the second time with Hitler as principal witness, but it subsequently became known that his wife had a criminal record for theft and prostitution. Fritsch was falsely accused of homosexual offences – on evidence conveniently produced by Himmler. This rather sordid episode provided Hitler with the perfect opportunity to subordinate the

army. The post of War Minister was abolished, and Hitler himself
became Commander-in-Chief of all armed forces with a personal high
command, the *Oberkommando der Wehrmacht* (OKW), headed by a
loyal adherent, General Keitel. The new Commander-in-Chief of the
army was General Brauchitsch – another compliant supporter of the
regime. In addition to these changes, a further 16 generals were retired
and 44 transferred.

   * There is little doubt that from 1938 the army's ability to shape
political developments within Germany was drastically reduced.
Whereas in the early years of the Nazi regime Hitler had correctly
recognised the need to work with the army leadership, by early 1938 he
was strong enough to mould it more closely to his requirements. That is
not to say, that it was without power, but merely that it had been tamed
to serve its new master. Thus, it was still generally recognised by the
opponents of Nazism that the army remained the one institution with
the technical means of striking successfully at the Nazi regime. For
example, it is now known that in the summer of 1938 a plan was drawn
up by a number of disillusioned generals to arrest Hitler in the event of
a full-scale European war breaking out over the Sudeten crisis.
However, from 1938 to 1942 Nazi diplomatic and military policy was so
successful that it effectively torpedoed the plans of those officers who
wished to organise military resistance. Moreover, once Germany found
itself at war again, resistance not only seemed treasonable, but also
smacked of a basic lack of patriotism in the face of the enemy.
   By early 1943 the military situation had changed dramatically. Defeat
in North Africa had been followed by the disaster of Stalingrad. Many
generals came to believe that the war could not be won, and yet the
army was continuing to fight on behalf of a regime which had
legitimised appalling atrocities and was now demanding 'total war'. It
was in this situation that a number of civilian resistance figures made
contact with dissident generals, such as Beck and Rommel, in order to
plan the assassination of Hitler and the creation of a provisional
government. Eventually, a bomb was placed by Colonel von Stauffen-
berg in Hitler's briefing room at his headquarters in East Prussia on 20
July 1944. The bomb exploded, but Hitler sustained only minor
injuries, and in the confused aftermath the generals in Berlin fatally
hesitated, thus enabling a group of loyal soldiers to arrest the conspir-
ators and re-establish order.
   * The failure of the 20 July plot marked the end of the powerful and
privileged position of the army in German society. Many officers were
among those arrested or executed in the brutal Gestapo enquiry which
followed. However, perhaps even more significant than this blood
purge, were the orders subsequently issued. The Nazi salute became
compulsory throughout the army; political officers were appointed to
oversee the indoctrination of the army; and finally, with Himmler's
appointment as Commander-in-Chief of the Home Army, the army was

brought under the control of the SS. The last traces of army independence had been subsumed within the Nazi regime.

Generally, historians have not been sympathetic to the role played by the German army during the Nazi years. Indeed, although one must avoid institutional stereotyping and recognise that there were different shades of opinion, it is difficult to avoid the conclusion that the army leadership played a naive and inept political game. Conditioned by their traditions of obedience, loyalty and patriotism, and encouraged by the authoritarian disposition of the Third Reich, the army became a vital mainstay of the Nazi regime in the early years. Yet, even when its own power to influence events had been drastically reduced in 1938 and the full implications of Nazi rule became apparent during the war, the army's leaders could not escape from their political and moral dilemma. The 20 July plot was a brave gesture, but the vacillation and indecision of that day were also indicative of the compromised position in which the army found itself by this time.

4 The Economics of the Third Reich

In the years before 1933 Hitler had been careful not to become tied down to the specific details of an economic policy. Despite the anti-capitalist sentiments of the 25 Point Programme, political realities necessitated a certain ambiguity in order to satisfy the different economic interest groups. However, it is equally clear that during 1932 the Nazi leadership began to consider more specifically a number of possible approaches to the issue of the economy. Firstly, there was the policy of autarky (economic self-sufficiency). This envisaged the creation of a trading or economic community under the dominating influence of Germany, which could be developed to rival the other great economic powers. Secondly, attention was given to the emerging idea of deficit financing, which found its most obvious expression in the theories of the British economist, John Maynard Keynes. By spending money on public works, it was intended to create jobs which would then act as an artificial stimulus to demand within the economy. Finally, there was the idea of the *Wehrwirtschaft* (defence economy), whereby Germany's peace-time economy was geared to the demands of total war, so as to avoid a repetition of the problems faced during the First World War when a long drawn out conflict on two fronts eventually caused economic collapse. However, despite the consideration given to such policies, no coherent plan had emerged by January 1933. Hitler had no interest in or understanding of economics. For him, it was merely the means to achieve his political and military ends. Consequently, although the three approaches described above all feature in the economic history of the Third Reich, there is a lack of consistency which suggests that economic policy tended to be pragmatic and to evolve out of the demands of the situation rather than being the result of careful planning. As one leading historian has stated, 'no single unified economic system prevailed throughout the entire period of the Nazi regime'.

  * In the early years Nazi economic policy was under the control of Hjalmar Schacht, President of the Reichsbank (1933–9), and Minister of Economics (1934–7). This reflected the need of the Nazi leadership to work with the powerful forces of big business, for Schacht was already a respected international financier because of his leading role in the creation of the new currency in the wake of the 1923 inflation. Under Schacht's guidance and influence, in the years 1933–6 government money was provided for various employment schemes – motorway construction, afforestation and public buildings. Subsidies helped to revitalise private building and repair work, and armaments expenditure was increased. Of course, it must be remembered that all this took place as the world economy began to recover. Nevertheless, the decline in unemployment to 1.7 million by the middle of 1935 was an impressive achievement – and one which won the Nazi regime admirers both at home and abroad.

  However, this success was also a contributory factor to two economic worries: the fear of rekindling inflation with growing demand, and the emergence of a balance of payments deficit as Germany imported more raw materials without increasing its exports. The problem of inflation never actually materialised because the regime established strict controls over prices and wages – an economic move facilitated by the political act of abolishing the trades unions in May 1933. However, a balance of payments problem first appeared in the summer of 1934 and was to recur regularly thereafter.

  The balance of payments problem was not merely an economic issue, for it carried with it large-scale political and military implications. If Germany was so short of foreign exchange, which sector of the economy was to have priority in spending the money? The Economics Minister, Schmitt, wanted to encourage public consumption in order to reduce unemployment. However, powerful voices in the armed forces and big business feared that this would limit the import of vital resources for the embryonic rearmament programme. Hitler could not ignore such pressure – especially as this economic problem coincided with the dilemma over the SA (see page 53). Consequently, Schmitt was removed, and Schacht combined the offices of Economics Minister and President of the Reichsbank.

  Schacht was not a Nazi, but his proven economic skills earned him the respect of the regime. Indeed, it has been claimed that Schacht 'contributed as much as Hitler to the construction of the Third Reich'. By a law of 3 July, he was given dictatorial powers over the economy, which he then used to introduce the 'New Plan' of September 1934. This provided for a comprehensive control by the government of all aspects of trade and currency exchange. In this way the government set the priorities. As a result, for example, in 1934 imports of raw cotton and wool were substantially cut in order to satisfy the import demands of heavy industry. Schacht also tried to promote trade and save foreign exchange by signing bilateral trade treaties, especially with the countries of south-east Europe and South America. These often took the form of straightforward barter agreements (thus avoiding the necessity of formal currency exchange). Alternatively, Germany agreed to purchase raw materials from such countries on the condition that the marks could only be used to buy back German goods (at one time it is estimated that the German mark had 237 different values depending on the country and the circumstances!). In this way Germany began to exert a powerful economic influence over the Balkans long before it obtained military and political control.

Schacht played a vital role by laying down the economic foundations of the Nazi state. By the end of 1935 Germany actually had a trade surplus, the unemployment rate was still falling, and overall industrial production had increased by 49.5 per cent since 1933. However, such successes masked fundamental structural weakneses. In many respects, as Schacht himself was only too aware, he had merely hidden the balance of payments problem by a series of clever financial disguises. In 1936 things came to a head over an impending crisis in Germany's balance of payments.

* Despite his economic 'tricks' and his apparent sympathy for deficit financing, Schacht believed that a budget deficit and a balance of payments could not be maintained indefinitely. In early 1936 it became clear to him that as the demands for rearmament and consumption increased, the German balance of payments would go deeply into the red. He therefore suggested a reduction in arms expenditure, in order to increase the production of industrial exports, which at least could be sold so as to earn foreign exchange. Such a solution had its adherents, especially in the export orientated industries, but it was unacceptable to the armed forces and to the Nazi leadership. Schacht's influence was on the wane.

The politico-economic crisis of 1936 was resolved by the introduction of the Four Year Plan under the control of Hermann Göring. Its aim was to make the German armed forces and economy ready for war within four years. In order to achieve this, the Plan highlighted four priorities: an increase in agricultural production, the retraining of key sectors of the labour force, government regulation of imports and exports, and, above all, the achievement of self-sufficiency in raw materials, such as oil, rubber and metals – if necesary by the development of synthetic substitutes. Such a programme marked an important turning-point in the Nazi regime. Nazi control over industry became much tighter, and Schacht found his influence much diminished, as he himself described in his book written in 1949:

1 Göring set out, with all the folly and incompetence of the
  amateur, to carry out the programme of economic self-
  sufficiency, or autarky, envisaged in the Four Year Plan. Hitler
  had given him as chief of the Four Year Plan operations in order
5 to extend his own influence over economic policy, which he did
  not find difficult, since he was now, of course, in a position to
  place really large contracts ... On December 17th 1936, Göring
  informed a meeting of big industrialists that it was no longer a
  question of producing economically, but simply of producing.
10 And as far as getting hold of foreign exchange was concerned it
  was quite immaterial whether the provisions of the law were
  complied with or not ... Göring's policy of recklessly exploiting
  Germany's economic substance necessarily brought me into more
  and more acute conflict with him, and for his part he exploited his
15 powers, with Hitler and the Party behind him, to counter my
  activity as Minister of Economics to an ever-increasing extent.

Schacht eventually resigned as Economics Minister in November
1937, and was replaced by the subservient Walther Funk. Thereafter,
Göring himself became the real economic dictator, and big business
found increasingly that it had to work within the framework laid down
by the Nazi leadership.

The success of the Plan was mixed. On the one hand it fell a long way
short of the targets in the vital commodities of rubber and oil, whilst
arms production never reached the levels desired by the armed forces
and Hitler. On the other hand, production of a number of key
materials, such as aluminium and explosives, had expanded greatly and
in others it had grown at a respectable rate. All in all Germany's reliance
on imports had not been exacerbated further, despite the economic
growth.

* By the end of 1938 German industrial production had increased by
105 per cent since 1933. Yet, Germany by no means possessed a war
economy. The research of BH Klein in the 1950s led him to argue that
this 'partial mobilisation' was a deliberate policy allied to the military
strategy of Blitzkrieg. In his view, Hitler and the armed forces
recognised Germany's precarious position over raw materials, and
consequently developed the strategy of short wars, which would not
excessively strain the economy. This also had the political advantage of
not reducing the production of consumer goods excessively. Klein
therefore argued that pre-1939 'the scale of Germany's economic
mobilisation for war was quite modest'. Indeed, he claimed, it was not
until the defeat at Stalingrad in the winter of 1942–3 that full economic
mobilisation began in earnest.

Klein's basic thesis has proved to be very influential, although it was
somewhat modified in the mid-1960s by Milward. He accepted that
Blitzkrieg was meant to avoid total war, but he also pointed out that 'no

nation had ever previously spent so vast a sum on preparations for war'. Moreover, he suggested that it was the German failure to take Moscow at the end of 1941, which was the real economic turning-point. By spring 1942 the German economic machine was ready for the war of attrition.

Such interpretations have now begun to be questioned. Prompted by the views of diplomatic historians, who see Hitler stumbling unintentionally into a major European war in September 1939, economic historians have started to revise their opinions about the direction and state of the German economy. Overy has argued forcefully that from the start Hitler envisaged a great conflict for world power and that this necessitated the transformation of the economy to the demands of total war. However, his preparations for this kind of war were intended to be finished by 1943. The war with Poland in 1939 was meant to be a local war, which Hitler wrongly believed would not involve Britain and France. The premature outbreak of continental conflict inevitably found the German economy only partially mobilised. But in Overy's opinion the underlying principles of Nazi economic policy were already clear. Since 1933 economic growth had been essentially directed to the needs of war, not civilian consumption. Between 1936 and 1939 over two-thirds of all German investment had gone into war-related projects. In a somewhat chilling conclusion Overy pointed out:

> 1 If war had been postponed until 1943–5 as Hitler had hoped, then Germany would have been much better prepared, and would also have had rockets, jet aircraft, inter-continental bombers, perhaps even atomic weapons. Though Britain and France did not know
> 5 it, declaring war in 1939 prevented Germany from becoming the super-power Hitler wanted. The drive for total war became instead *Blitzkrieg* by default.

The controversy about the relationship between economic policy and military strategy also helps us to understand the changing balance of power in the politics of the Third Reich. From 1933 the position of the business community began to improve. Helped by the upturn in world trade, and encouraged by the Nazi destruction of the free trade unions, a commercial recovery was set in motion. However, despite all the Nazi electoral promises, small business found itself being squeezed out by the power of big business, whose support the Nazis needed for rearmament. Consequently, it was the giant coal and steel industries which prospered most initially; however, from 1936 and the introduction of the Four Year Plan it was the electro-chemicals sector that benefited most, largely because of its links with armaments production. In particular, the huge corporation IG Farben, which led the way in the development of synthetic substitutes, saw its profits increase from 71m Reichsmarks in 1935 to 240m Reichsmarks in 1939.

* Amidst all this controversy, what cannot be doubted is that the military successes achieved by the armed forces by the summer of 1941 not only won Hitler and the regime valuable popular support, but also conveniently disguised such economic problems as the shortage of raw materials, the need to ration food from September 1939 and the general inefficiency of the bureaucracy co-ordinating military and economic policies. For, despite the image of German order and efficiency, British economic mobilisation for war was much quicker in the years 1939–41.

Table 2
GNP and military expenditure in Germany and Britain

	Germany (billions of RM)			Britain (billions of £)		
	GNP	Military expenditure	%	GNP	Military expenditure	%
1938	105	17.2	17	4.8	0.4	8
1939	130	30.0	23	5.0	1.1	22
1940	141	53.0	38	6.0	3.2	53
1941	152	71.0	47	6.8	4.1	60

It is perhaps because of Hitler's lack of interest in economic affairs that historians find it difficult to pin-point exactly when the Nazi regime started to tackle its economic weaknesses. Fritz Todt, appointed Minister of Armaments in March 1940, certainly initiated and prepared many of the reforms attributed to Albert Speer, who succeeded him in February 1942. Speer also enjoyed excellent personal relations with Hitler, and he used the Führer's authority to push through his economic programme.

Todt and Speer advocated a policy of 'industrial self-responsibility'. The controls and constraints previously placed upon business, in order to subject it to Nazi wishes, were relaxed. In their place was established a Central Planning Board. It had a number of committees, each representing one vital sector of the economy. In this way Speer maintained overall control of the war economy, whilst allowing the industrialists a considerable degree of freedom. From 1942 arms production increased markedly, reaching its highest levels in the latter half of 1944.

However, such economic 'successes' could not reverse the declining military situation. By the end of 1944 Allied forces were advancing from both east and west, and the German war economy degenerated rapidly. The breakdown of communications, the shortage of vital raw materials and a lack of labour meant that the war could not be continued effectively. Yet, to the very end German industry continued to work with the Nazi regime. Leaders of big business were not to be found amongst the plotters of 20 July 1944. Perhaps this was because for those involved in the production of armaments the material benefits were just too attractive. Profits continued to increase, and this was reason enough to collaborate with the regime. However, that is not say that they ever directed policy. From 1936 this was clearly determined by the Nazi leadership.

5 Conclusion

To describe the Third Reich as 'totalitarian' is not inaccurate. However, it is possibly misleading as it is a term which is very much a product of the post-1945 Cold War, when liberal western historians rather too readily assumed an identity between Hitler's Germany, Stalin's Russia and Mussolini's Italy. Even more dubious was the attempt by Soviet and East German historians (in the pre-Gorbachev era) to portray the Nazi state as simply the political manifestation of a powerful capitalist elite. Both interpretations have become inadequate explanations of the power structure in the Third Reich.

The totalitarian model of Nazi Germany can be criticised on two major counts. Although Germany was politically a one-party state, the Nazi Party did not have the organisation or unity of purpose to dominate affairs (unlike the Bolsheviks in the USSR). Secondly, in no way did the Nazis ever establish a centralised command control over the economy (in direct contrast to the situation in USSR). Nazi Germany was not the monolithic structure suggested by the term totalitarian. Equally, however, the continued existence of private enterprise and the obvious sympathy of certain elements of big business for the regime in no way amounts to an acceptance of the traditional Marxist view. For, in reality, it is only possible to sustain the thesis that economic forces predominated at the expense of other power blocs by ignoring much of the available evidence.

Instead, historians have accepted the view that the Third Reich in its power structure was a 'polycracy' – an alliance of different blocs, which, although not in unison, were dependent on each other and prepared to work with each other as partners in power. The most important of these blocs would seem to have been the Nazi Party itself, the SS-Police-SD system, the army, big business and, to some extent, the higher levels of the state bureaucracy (although even this picture is over-simplified and disguises the divisions and conflicts within these various groups). At the centre of all this there was the dominating presence of Hitler himself.

However, even this picture is too basic, since the relationship between these 'power blocs' was far from static. In the early years, Hitler and the Nazis – at this stage the SS-Police-SD system was relatively insignificant – were heavily dependent upon the sympathy of the army and big business, and so they did not attempt to control them directly because they feared alienating them. Indeed, the destruction of the SA in 1934 was motivated very much by the need to placate the traditional vested interests, and it was seen as a blow by many in the Party. At this stage, the rearmament programme also acted as a powerful focus of common interest – contracts and profits for industry, restored prestige for the army, and foundations being laid for the future imperial expansion planned by the Nazis.

All this changed in the course of 1936–8. Hitler's personal political position was by this time much stronger and was ruthlessly supported by the emerging power of Himmler's SS-Police-SD system. Hitler was therefore less constrained by the need for political compromise and could afford to pursue his objectives more directiy. Consequently, the economic crisis of 1936 led to the disappearance of Schacht and the introduction of the Four Year Plan under Göring intended to create a war economy. This represented a major shift in the balance of power away from big business as a whole, although it was strongly supported by the electro-chemicals sector because of its links with arms production. Despite the fact that the army had sided with the Nazi leadership in 1936, it was also severely weakened two years later by the purge of major generals after Blomberg and Fritsch had expressed their doubts about the direction of Hitler's foreign policy.

By 1938, therefore, both the army and big business had been reduced to the role of junior partners in the Third Reich's power structure. This weakening of their positions was to continue in subsequent years, although at first the army gained great kudos from the military victories of 1939–41. However, it was under the pressures of war that the power and influence of the SS-Police-SD system was able to grow so enormously and to become the dominant power bloc. Indeed, some historians have gone as far as to refer to the emergence of the 'SS state'. This also coincided with the weakening of the traditional elites within the state bureaucracy as the Party apparatus under Bormann's influence began to exert a relatively greater influence. It would seem therefore that by the time of the Third Reich's eventual demise the various organs of Nazism had progressively assumed a more and more dominant role to the detriment of external agencies.

Structuralist historians have certainly succeeded in highlighting a lack of planning and organisation on Hitler's part, so that it is now generally appreciated that divisions and rivalries in the government of the Third Reich persisted throughout its 12 year life. Both Himmler and Göring headed their own institutional empires and their aims and interests often brought them into conflict not only with each other, but also with other leading Nazis. Likewise, Speer and Sauckel (Plenipotentiary for Labour) clashed continuously over the direction of labour in the war economy. Whilst Bormann and Goebbels were both so despised within the Party that personal rivalries and ambitions often dominated at the expense of efficient government. Yet, despite all this talk of individual and institutional confrontation, it is difficult to ignore Hitler or to accept the view of him as a 'weak dictator' (excepting perhaps the last few months of his life). Hitler created the Party and headed a regime which was built upon the very principle of authoritarian leadership. It is impossible to pin-point any major domestic development which was contrary to Hitler's wishes. Equally, it was Hitler's own views on continental conquest and racial supremacy which determined Germany's foreign and military policy. In the final analysis, it is surely indicative that the SS-Police-SD complex emerged as *the* dominant power bloc, and that its guiding principle from the start had been unquestioning obedience to the will of the *Führer*.

OATH   OR   LOYALTY TO THE FUHRER.

Making notes on 'Politics and Economics in the Nazi State, 1933–45'

There are many common misapprehensions about the Nazi state. Your notes on this chapter should give you a good insight into the more complex realities. Make certain you understand the relevant political and economic terminology. Above all, keep two questions in mind throughout:

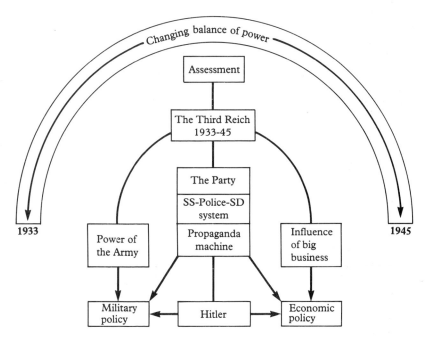

Summary – Politics and Economics in the Nazi State, 1933-45

i) How did the various political and economic forces in the Third
Reich *relate* to each other?
ii) How did the relationship between them change over time?
The following headings, sub-headings and questions should assist you:

1   Totalitarianism
1.1   What do you understand by the term totalitarianism?
2   The Nazi System of Government
2.1   Party and state.
2.1.1 What was the theoretical relationship between Party and state?
2.1.2 Why did the Party find it so difficult to establish a power-base
within the Third Reich?
2.1.3 The influence of Hess and Bormann. How did they change the
position of the Party?
2.2   The role of Hitler.
2.2.1 What were the practical constraints on Hitler's theoretical position of supreme power?
2.2.2 'Structuralist' and 'intentionalist' interpretations of Hitler's position.
2.3   The apparatus of the police state.
2.3.1 Origins, development and growth of the SS.
2.3.2 How significant was the position of the SS in the Third Reich?
2.4   The Nazi propaganda machine.
2.4.1 Broadcasting.
2.4.2 Press.
3   The army
3.1   Why was the position of the army especially significant in the
political life of Germany?
3.2   Summarise the relationship of the army to the Nazi regime in
each of the following periods: 1933–4; 1934–8; 1938–44; and
1944–5.
3.3   Why has the role of the German army been the focus of such
criticism?
4   The Economics of the Third Reich
4.1   Economic influences on the Nazis.
4.2   The policy of Schacht. How did he lay the economic foundations
of the Third Reich?
4.3   The Four Year Plan. Why was the crisis of 1936 such a
significant economic and political turning-point?
4.4   A war economy? Arguments for and against.
4.5   The economic impact of war.
5   Conclusion

Answering essay questions on 'Politics and Economics in the Nazi State, 1933–45'

In this chapter you have looked at the political structure of the Third Reich in its broadest sense and, although you might be asked a very specific question on any one aspect of it, it is much more likely that you will be confronted with questions inviting a broad analysis of the Nazi state; therefore it may well be necessary to embrace material from chapter 4 as well.

Many of the questions fall into the 'to what extent' category. Although such questions may be phrased with a point of focus, they all require you to construct a two-part answer. The first part will examine the points in favour of the proposition and the second part will discuss those against it. Consider these questions:

1 To what extent would you agree with the description of the Third Reich as the 'SS state'?
2 To what extent was the Party the most vital element in the Nazi state?
3 How far did the Nazis change the political structure of Germany?
4 To what extent was Nazi Germany controlled by the dictatorial leadership of Adolf Hitler?
5 To what extent was the Third Reich built upon the use of political terror?
6 How valid is the term 'totalitarian' as a description of the Third Reich?

Each of these questions requires you to weigh the significance of the proposition against the other contributory factors. For example, question 2 asks you to assess the importance of the Party in the Nazi state, so by implication you must also analyse other 'elements' in order to reach a conclusion. What other elements would you need to discuss? Remember that the majority of your time should be devoted to a consideration of the importance of the Party. The question is not an invitation to you to discuss the Nazi state in general.

Now prepare an essay plan for question 4 based around the following sub-questions:
   a) In what ways did Hitler exert control in the Third Reich?
   b) In what ways did he fail to exert control?
   c) Who/What also exerted control?
Finally, write out your conclusion in full. This will be a difficult task if it is done properly because you will be trying to integrate all the evidence into a crisp and coherent statement. However, doing it will certainly help to clarify your thoughts on the topic.

Source based questions on 'Politics and Economics in the Nazi State, 1933–45'

1 The Role of Hitler

Read the extracts on Hitler's constitutional position and his daily routine on page 64. Answer the following questions:

a) According to Nazi constitutional theory what was the basis of the *Führer*'s power? (**3 marks**)

b) Why do you think the position of *Führer* was not portrayed as a state office? (**3 marks**)

c) What major political failings are highlighted in the description of Hitler's lifestyle? (**4 marks**)

d) Why do you think the regime went to the trouble of producing such verbose constitutional theory? (**4 marks**)

e) What are the strengths and weaknesses of both these extracts for the student of Hitler's Germany? (**6 marks**)

2 Nazi Attitudes to Propaganda

Read the two extracts from Goebbels on propaganda on page 68. Answer the following questions:

a) Explain in your own words Goebbels' major aims as Minister of Propaganda. (**3 marks**)

b) Why did Goebbels place so much importance on the control of the radio? (**3 marks**)

c) How do you think Goebbels might have justified the Nazi monopoly of the radio? (**4 marks**)

d) To what extent did the propaganda machine succeed in deluding the people from the reality of life in the Third Reich? (**5 marks**)

3 Nazi Economics

Read the extracts from Schacht (page 76) and Overy (page 77) and then study the table of statistics on page 78. Answer the following questions:

a) What are Schacht's major criticisms of Nazi economic policy from 1936? (**3 marks**)

b) In what ways should Schacht's analysis be treated with caution? Why is it still a very useful source for the historian? (**5 marks**)

c) Explain in your own words how and why Overy's analysis of economic policy dovetails with German foreign policy from 1936 to 1941. (**5 marks**)

d) In what ways could you criticise the presentation of the statistics? (**4 marks**)

e) Do these sources, and other evidence known to you, support the thesis that 'Nazi economic policy made a war of conquest inevitable'? (**8 marks**)

4 The Structure of the Third Reich

Study the painting by Zeller on page 67 and the poster on the front cover. Answer the following questions:

a) What impression of Hitler is the artist trying to create in the poster? Explain your answer. (**4 marks**)

b) To what extent does the poster's slogan accurately reflect Nazi ideology? (**5 marks**)

c) Zeller's painting was entitled 'Hitler's State'. What is the image of the Third Reich as projected by the artist? (**7 marks**)

d) Despite the differences between the two sources, what similaritities can you detect in the way they portray the structure of the Third Reich? (**4 marks**)

CHAPTER 6

The Social Impact of the Third Reich

1 Nazi Views on Society

Hitler always claimed that National Socialism was more than just a political party. It was a movement and an ideology that aimed to exercise power so as to transform German society. It recoiled against the prevailing values of liberal individualism and socialist class warfare, and in their place it upheld the concept of *Volksgemeinschaft*, or people's community. By trying to bridge class and social divisions this idea had become an important element in electoral propaganda (see also page 20). However, once in power it meant the application of Nazi ideas on race and struggle into everyday life by the encouragement of new social attitudes and the enforcement of racial principles throughout society. In effect, membership of the *Volksgemeinschaft* was open to those Aryans, of a healthy physical and mental condition (war cripples excepted), who were prepared to accept the constraints of dictatorship. However, it is difficult to go beyond these rather nebulous intimations of Nazi social ideology, and to identify with any real clarity what Nazi society was actually intended to be like. There were too many contradictions and uncertainties, both in the theory and practice of its social policy. In this chapter you will be looking at the impact of the Third Reich upon different aspects of society. As you read it, try to assess what was changed and what remained unchanged within German society. Above all, consider whether Hitler's Germany was socially reactionary or revolutionary.

2 Material Conditions

On a very general level the revival of the economy (in conjunction with Hitler's diplomatic successes) contributed greatly to the German people's acceptance, or at least tolerance, of the regime. In the pre-war years it really did seem to many Germans as if the Nazis had pulled their country out of the economic quagmire. However, in material terms the effects varied considerably from one class to another.

For the industrial working class there were the positive benefits of regular work, stable rents and recreational provision organised by the Nazi KDF (*Kraft durch Freude* – Strength through Joy), which made very real opportunities available to millions of workers – cultural visits, sports facilities and holiday travel. However, against these advantages must be set the loss of industrial bargaining rights and the demands placed on workers by management and by the government, which intervened to control pay increases and to limit workers' freedom of movement. From May 1933 workers had no real option but to join the

NAZIS = NATIONAL SOCIALISM

DAF (*Deutsche Arbeitsfront* – German Labour Front) and accept its stipulations on working conditions. The analysis of workers' wages has proved to be a particularly complicated issue, mainly because there are so many variables to take into account, such as age, occupation and geographical location. However, the average worker's real wages (the actual purchasing power after taking into account the inflation rate) only rose above 1929 levels in 1938. Moreover, the average working week had increased from 43 hours in 1933 to 47 hours in 1939. Despite all the complications, it is clear that this generalised picture disguises one definite point of differentiation: the best gains were made by those in industries associated with the rearmament boom, while those in consumer goods struggled to maintain their real incomes.

The farming community had been attracted to the Nazi cause by the promise of economic aid and by the apparent sympathy of National Socialism for its role in society. The Nazi ideology of 'Blood and Soil' portrayed the peasantry as racially the purest element of the *Volk*, and as representative of those traditional values which were being lost in the amorphous urban society of industrial Germany. Yet, economic realities meant that in practice the impact of Nazi policy was rather mixed. Certainly, a substantial number of farm debts were written off, and all farmers benefited from an increase in prices betweeen 1933 and 1936. However, the Reich Food Estate, established in 1933, controlled every aspect of agricultural production and consumption, and its bureaucratic meddling became the focus of much resentment (each hen, it was stipulated, had to lay 65 eggs per year!). Even the *Reich Entailed Farm Law* of 1933, which gave security of tenure to the owners of medium-sized farms between 7.5 and 125 hectares, was resented. This was because, since it forbade the division of farms, farmers faced a very real problem in providing a future for more than one of their children. Indeed, by the late 1930s, despite the regime's desire to increase agricultural production, it was clear that there had been a significant drift of workers to the towns where wages were higher. German agriculture just did not have the economic power to compete with other sectors of the economy and, as there were limits to Nazi interventionism and economic regulation, it faced a severe shortage of labour.

Another social class which expected to benefit from the Nazi regime was the *Mittelstand*. Yet, its position continued to decline under the Nazis, since only a very limited attempt was made to implement the electoral promises. The harsh commercial realities of the 1930s, together with the Nazi preference for big business, whose support was required for rearmament, simply perpetuated the trend of relative economic decline which went back to the beginnings of Germany's industrialisation. In 1933 20 per cent of the owners of *Mittelstand* businesses were under 30 years old and 14 per cent over 60. By 1939 the corresponding figures were 10 per cent and 19 per cent. The truth is that the *Mittelstand* found itself squeezed out as a result of changing economic conditions which were completely beyond its control and about which the Nazi government was not prepared to regulate now that it needed to maintain the sympathies of those economic interest groups involved in arms production.

As we have already seen, it was big business (see page 77) which benefited most from the economic programme of the Nazis. Despite a range of government controls, the financial gains were impressive. The value of German industry steadily increased, as shown by the rise in the share index from 41 points in 1932 to 106 in 1940, whilst dividends to investors grew from an average 2.83 per cent to 6.60 per cent over the same period. Such growth was also reflected in the improved salaries of management – from an average 3700RM in 1934 to 5420RM in 1938.

3 Anti-Semitism

At the very centre of Nazi social policy was the issue of race, and by extension, anti-Semitism. Hitler's obsessive hatred of the Jews was perhaps the most dominant and consistent theme of his political career. The translation of such ideas into actual policy was to lead to economic boycotts, racial laws, government inspired violence and pogroms, and finally, to the obscenities of mass-shootings and the gas-chambers. This is not the place for a detailed factual account of such episodes, although table 3 on pages 89–90 does give a brief chronology. Rather, it is more important to think about the key issues raised by the Nazi racial policy, which eventually culminated in genocide – or as it has more commonly become known 'the Holocaust'. In particular, how was it possible for the state apparatus of a civilised and advanced nation to effect such a policy? And to what extent was this policy a result of the long-cherished aim of Hitler alone? For historians, such questions pose immense problems. The detached rational objectivity required of historical analysis is exceedingly difficult to achieve when the subject is of itself so emotive, so fantastic and in many respects so irrational. And yet, such questions cannot be ignored.

Anti-Semitism has a long-established tradition in European history: it was not the preserve of the Nazis, and it certainly has never been just a purely German phenomenon. It was rooted in the religious hostility of Christendom towards the Jews (as the murderers of Jesus) which can be traced back many centuries. Yet, there emerged in Germany in the course of the nineteenth century a more clearly defined anti-Semitism, which was based upon racism and social resentment. By 1900 a number of specifically anti-Semitic political parties were winning seats in the *Reichstag* and, although they were comparatively few, anti-Semitic ideas were becoming more prevalent and generally more respectable. Some historians have seen this anti-Semitism as a by-product of the nationalist passions stirred up by unification and the emergence of Germany as a world power. However, it should be remembered that a

Table 3
Chronology of Jewish Persecution, 1933–45

1933	1 April	First official boycott of Jewish shops and professions.
	7 April	Law for the Restoration of the Professional Civil Service. Excluded Jews from government jobs.
1934		Various laws prohibit Jews from the professions.
1935	15 September	Nuremberg Race Laws: 1) Reich Citizenship Act. 'A citizen of the Reich is that subject only who is of German or kindred blood'. 2) Law for the Protection of German Blood and German Honour. Marriages between Jews and German citizens forbidden. Extra-marital relations between Jews and German citizens forbidden.
1936	Summer	Decline in anti-semitic campaign because of Berlin Olympics.
1937		Intensification of Aryanization programme in commerce and professions.
1938	28 October	Expulsion of 17,000 Polish Jews resident in Germany.
	7 November	Assassination of Ernst von Rath, a diplomatic offficial at the German Embassy in Paris by Herschel Grünspan, a Jew.
	9 November	*Kristallnacht* (Crystal Night), pogrom throughout Germany. Destruction of Jewish shops, homes and synagogues. 100 Jews killed and 20,000 sent to concentration camps.
	15 November	Expulsion of all Jewish pupils from schools.
	3 December	Compulsory closure and sale of all Jewish businesses.
1939	30 April	Confiscation of all Jewish valuables.
	1 September	Introduction of curfew for Jews.
1940		First deportations of Jews from certain German provinces.
1941	June	*Einsatzgruppen* (Action squads) of SS

		moved into Russia behind the advancing armies to round up and kill Jews.
1941	1 September	All Jews forced to wear the Yellow Star of David. — *IDENTIFICATION*
1942	20 January	Wannsee Conference. Meeting of various government and Party agencies agreed to the 'Final Solution' of the Jewish problem.
	Spring	Extermination facilities established at Auschwitz, Chelmno, Majdanek and Treblinka.
1943	February	Destruction of Warsaw Ghetto.
	Summer	Transportation of Jews from all over German-occupied Europe to death camps begun. Death of approximately 6 million Jews.
1945	26 January	Liberation of Auschwitz by Soviet troops.

similar development had also taken place in German-speaking Austria, and there the political situation was very different.

In reality, the emergence of political anti-Semitism was a response to intellectual developments and changing sociological conditions. The Jews became an easy scapegoat for the discontent and disorientation felt by many people as rapid industrialisation and urbanisation took place. The Jewish community was easily identifiable because of its different traditions, and the focus of envy because it was viewed as privileged. In 1933, for example, although Jews comprised less than one percent of the German population, they composed more than 16 per cent of lawyers, 10 per cent of doctors and 5 per cent of editors and writers. In the late nineteenth century anti-Semitism also began to be presented in a more intellectual vein by the application of racial theories of Social Darwinism. In this way an aura of intellectual respectability was given to those anti-Semites who portrayed the Jews as an 'inferior' or 'parasitic' race. One leading historian of Nazi Germany has claimed that by 1914, 'in the form of a basic dislike of the Jews and of what they were felt to represent, it [anti-Semitism] had succeeded in permeating broad sections of German society from the Kaiser down to the lower middle class. Ominously, it was particularly strongly entrenched within the academic community, thereby influencing the next generation.'

It was in such an environment that Hitler's personal anti-Semitism developed. He was the product, not the creator, of a society which was permeated by such prejudices. However, it would be inaccurate to dismiss Hitler as just another anti-Semite. Hitler's hatred of Jews was obsessive and vindictive, and it shaped his whole political philosophy.

Without his personal commitment to attack the Jews and without his charismatic skills as a political leader, it seems unlikely that anti-Semitism could have become such an integral part of the Nazi movement. That he was able to do this can only be explained by the unique circumstances of post-war Germany: the self-deception of the 'stab in the back'; the humiliation of Versailles; the political weakness of the Weimar Republic; and the extreme socio-economic problems of 1918–23 and 1929–33. In such a situation, Hitler was able to exploit latent hostility towards the Jews and turn it into a radical doctrine of hatred.

However, the appointment of an anti-Semite as Chancellor, even if he did enjoy 37.3 per cent of the popular vote, cannot on its own explain the events of 1933–45. Indeed, in a 1934 survey into the reasons why people joined the Nazis, over 60 per cent did not even mention anti-Semitism. How then was it possible to translate the rhetoric of Nazi anti-Semitism into the brutal policy of 1933–45?

At first the Nazi approach was gradualist. The early moves against the Jews gave no suggestion of the end result. Indeed, for some Germans the boycotts and discriminatory legislation were no more than the Jews deserved. For the more liberally-minded, who found such action offensive, there was the practical problem of how to show opposition and to offer resistance. Once the apparatus of dictatorship was well-established by the end of 1934, the futility of opposition was apparent to most people. Feelings of hopelessness were increasingly superseded by those of fear. To show sympathy or to protect the Jews was to risk one's own freedom or one's own life. It was an unenviable dilemma. Another explanation of popular reactions is offered by Melita Maschmann in her memoirs:

1 I had learned from the example of my parents that one could have anti-Semitic opinions without this interfering in one's personal relations with individual Jews. There may be a vestige of tolerance in this attitude, but it is really just this confusion which
5 I blame for the fact that I later contrived to dedicate body and soul to an inhuman political system, without this giving me doubts about my own individual decency. In preaching that all the misery of the nations was due to the Jews or that the Jewish spirit was seditious and Jewish blood corrupting, I was not
10 compelled to think of you or old Herr Lewy or Rosel Cohn: I thought only of the bogy-man, 'The Jew'. And when I heard that the Jews were being driven from their professions and homes and imprisoned in ghettos, the points switched automatically in my mind to steer me round the thought that such a fate could also
15 overtake you or old Lewy. It was only *the* Jew who was being persecuted and 'made harmless'.

SPEAK OF JEWS LIKE A
CONTAGEOUS DISEASE.

As for the Jewish community itself, the persecution did lead to the emigration of nearly 150,000 people (nearly 30 per cent of the 1933 Jewish population) between 1933 and 1938. But the majority preferred to take their chance in Germany, rather than lose their homes and possessions by leaving.

It is of course the inconceivable nature of events after 1939 which partially explain why the holocaust was possible. Who in 1939 could have predicted the scenario of the next six years? The suggestion that millions would be systematically exterminated would have defied belief. It is an event in modern European history which even now is almost beyond rational comprehension; for those who lived in occupied Europe it was easier and more comfortable to dismiss the rumours as gross and macabre exaggerations – the result of war-time gossip and allied propaganda.

Yet, the unbelievable did happen, and it required not only the passivity of the 'innocent' majority but also the actions of a 'criminal' minority. Of course, there were the Party fanatics, such as Heydrich, Eichmann and Himmler, who genuinely believed in the righteousness of the 'Final Solution'. In October 1943 Himmler spoke to a group of SS commanders in occupied Poland:

1 I want to speak here before you in all openness about a very delicate subject. Among us it should be talked about quite openly, but despite this we shall never talk about it in public. I mean the evacuation of the Jews, the extermination of the Jewish
5 people. This is one of those things that one says easily enough. 'The Jewish people will be exterminated' says many a party comrade. 'OK – stands in the programme – elimination of Jews – extermination – we'll do it' . . . Of all the people that talk that way, none has seen it happen, none has been through it. Most of
10 you know what it means when 100 corpses are lying together, when 500 are lying there, or when 1000 are lying there. To have seen that through and while doing so – leaving aside exceptions owing to human weakness – to have maintained our integrity, that has made us hard. This is an unwritten and never-to-be written
15 page of glory in our history.

Equally, there were probably some real psychopaths and sadists (as in any society) who enjoyed the blood-letting. However, the reality is that most of the SS involved in running the camps were ordinary young men, brutalised by war, but somehow convinced that what they were doing was part of a higher mission. It is their normality and their preparedness to accept orders which is so frightening. In his auto-biography, completed shortly before his execution, Rudolf Höss, the commandant at Auschwitz, wrote:

Executors were simply "normal people – drawn by washed Hitlers policies

1 I had to appear cold and indifferent to events which must have wrung the heart of anyone possessed of human feelings ... I had to watch coldly while the mothers with laughing or crying children went to the gas-chambers ... I had to see everything. I
5 had to watch hour by hour, by night and by day, the burning and the removal of the bodies, the extraction of the teeth, the cutting of the hair, the whole grisly business ... I had to do all this, because I was the one to whom everyone looked, because I had to show them all that I did not merely issue the orders and make the
10 regulations but was also prepared to be present at whatever task I had assigned to my subordinates ... In the face of such grim considerations I was forced to bury all human considerations as deeply as possible ... I had to observe everything with a cold indifference ... In Auschwitz, I truly had no reason to complain
15 that I was bored ... I had only one end in view, to drive everyone and everything forward, so that I could accomplish the measures laid down ... Every German had to commit himself heart and soul, so that we might win the war ... By the will of the *Reichsführer* SS, Auschwitz became the greatest human exter-
20 mination centre of all time.

It is a poignant and revealing insight into a man, who personally admitted responsibility for the death of at least 1,250,000 human beings.

In all of this, one key question still dividing historians is the exact role of Hitler, and it relates back to the interpretational controversy of 'intentionalist' and 'structuralist' discussed earlier. For historians of the 'intentionalist' school, Hitler remains the key. He is seen as having committed himself to the extermination of the Jews at an early stage in his political career, and then followed a consistent policy which led logically from the persecution of 1933 to the gates of Auschwitz. In its simplest form they suggest that the holocaust happened because Hitler willed it. On the other hand, historians of the 'structuralist' school reject the idea of a long-term plan for mass-extermination. Rather, the 'Final Solution', it is suggested, came to be implemented as a result of an inner momentum within the regime – a result of the chaotic nature of government in which various institutions and individuals improvised a policy out of the chaotic military and human situation in eastern Europe by the end of 1941. According to such interpretations, moral responsibility for the 'Final Solution' extends beyond Hitler to the apparatus of the polycratic regime (nearly all 'structuralist' historians emphasise that this in no way reduces the guilt of Hitler himself, who was in total agreement with such a policy). Mommsen, for example, concluded his analysis as follows: 'It cannot be proved, for instance, that Hitler himself gave the order for the Final Solution, though this does not mean that he did not approve the policy. That the solution was

'Entry to Block 11', Auschwitz, 1943 by W. Siwek

put into effect is by no means to be ascribed to Hitler alone, but to the complexity of the decision-making process in the Third Reich, which brought about a progressive and cumulative radicalisation'.

In Germany the moral dimension has helped to make this historical debate a particularly lively one. Indeed, this aspect of its past remains central to the dilemma of modern Germany's identity as a nation. However, the controversy is also rooted in the evidence and its interpretation. Certainly, no written order from Hitler for the killing of the Jews has ever been found; but that does not prove that there never was such an order, either written or verbal. Clearly, Hitler spoke in violent and barbaric terms about the Jews from an early stage in his political career. But it would be fallacious to assume from the stand-point of 1945 that genocide was therefore the intention from the start. And, although it does seem that the initial arrangements for the implementation of the 'Final Solution' indicate a haphazard and makeshift approach, it should be remembered that this was typical of much of the Third Reich, and it does not necessarily negate the all important and all-pervasive influence of Hitler.

4 Education and Youth

What is the purpose of education? It is a question you might ask yourself, for it invites any number of replies. The aims of education have varied greatly over time and from one society to another. In Nazi Germany education became merely a tool for the long-term survival of the Nazi system. In a somewhat chilling statement (threat?) Hitler expressed his views in 1933:

> 1 When an opponent declares, 'I will not come over to your side', I
> calmly say, 'Your child belongs to us already . . . What are you?
> You will pass on. Your descendants, however, now stand in the
> new camp. In a short time they will know nothing else but this
> 5 new community'.

Education in the Third Reich was therefore intended to indoctrinate its youth so completely in the principles and ethos of National Socialism that the long-term survival of the 'New Order' would never be brought into question:

> 1 National Socialism is an ideology whose claim to validity is total
> and does not wish to be subject to the random formation of
> opinion. The means of implementing this claim is through
> education. German youth must no longer – as in the Liberal era in
> 5 the cause of so-called objectivity – be confronted with the choice
> of whether it wishes to grow up in a spirit of materialism or
> idealism, of racism or internationalism, of religion or godlessness,

but it must be consciously shaped according to the principles
which are recognised as correct and which have shown themselves
10 to be correct: according to the principles of the ideology of
National Socialism.

(National Socialist Teachers' League official in 1937)

[handwritten: long term survival of the Nazi party.]

This was to be achieved not only through the traditional structure of the
educational system, but also by the development of various Nazi youth
movements. How then did the Nazi regime 'educate' Germany's youth
and to what extent was it successful?

* The actual organisation of the state educational system was not
fundamentally altered, although by a law of 1934 control was wrested
from the *Länder* and centralised under the Reich Ministry of Education
and Science. The Ministry was then able to adapt the existing system to
suit Nazi purposes by introducing a number of internal changes.
Firstly, the teaching profession itself was 'reconditioned': politically
unreliable individuals were removed; special courses were arranged for
those teachers who remained unconvinced by the new requirements;
and the influence and interference of the NSLB (*Nationalsozialistische
Lehrerbund* – National Socialist Teachers' League) continued to increase, so that by 1937 it included 97 per cent of all teachers. Secondly,
the curricula and syllabi were adapted. A much greater emphasis was
placed on physical education, so that 15 per cent of school time was
given over to it, and games teachers assumed an increased status and
importance in the school hierarchy. On the academic front, German,
Biology and History were the focus of special attention. The study of
German language and literature was intended to create 'a consciousness
of being German', and to inculcate a martial and nationalistic spirit.
Amongst the list of suggested reading for 14-year-old pupils was a book
entitled *The Battle of Tannenberg*, which included the following extract:
'A Russian soldier tried to bar the infiltrator's way, but Otto's bayonet
slid gratingly between the Russian's ribs, so that he collapsed groaning.
There it lay before him, simple and distinguished, his dream's desire,
the Iron Cross'. Biology became the means by which to deliver Nazi
racial theory: ethnic classification, population policy and racial genetics
were all integrated into the syllabus. Not surprisingly, History was also
given a special place in the Nazi curriculum:

1 The German nation in its essence and greatness, in its fateful
struggle for internal and external identity is the subject of history.
It is based on the natural bond of the child with his nation and, by
interpreting history as the fateful struggle for existence between
5 the nations, has the particular task of educating young people to
respect the great German past and to have faith in the mission and
future of their own nation and to respect the right of existence of
other nations. The teaching of history must bring the past alive

for the young German in such a way that it enables him to
10 understand the present, makes him feel the responsibility of every
individual for the nation as a whole and gives him encouragement
for his own political activity. It will thereby awaken in the
younger generation that sense of responsibility towards ancestors
and grandchildren which will enable it to let its life be subsumed
15 in eternal Germany . . .

A new understanding of the German past has emerged from the
faith of the National Socialist movement in the future of the
German people. The teaching of history must come from this vital
faith, it must fill young people with the awareness that they
20 belong to a nation which of all the European nations had the
longest and most difficult path to its unification but now, at the
beginning of a new epoch, can look forward to what is coming full
of confidence.

(German Central Institute of Education, 1938)

One final innovation was the creation of various types of elite school,
which were intended to prepare the best of Germany's youth for future
political leadership. The 21 *Napolas* (National Political Educational
Institutions) and the 10 Adolf Hitler Schools, both for boys of
secondary school age, and the 3 *Ordensburgen*, for boys of college age,
all emphasised physical training, para-military activities and political
education.

* However, it was the youth movements which assumed the real
responsibility for the development of the vast majority of German
youth. There was a long and well-established tradition of youth
organisation in Germany, but in 1933 the Hitler Youth represented
only 1 per cent of the total. In the next six years its structure and
membership grew remarkably.

	Table 4			
	Nazi Youth Movements			
	1932	1934	1936	1938
DJ	28,600	1,457,300	1,785,400	2,064,500
HJ	55,400	786,000	1,168,700	1,663,300
JM	4,700	862,300	1,610,000	1,855,100
BDM	19,200	471,900	873,100	1,448,300
Total	108,000	3,577,600	5,437,600	7,031,200
Total no. of 10–18 yr olds	–	7,682,000	8,656,000	9,109,000

DJ = *Deutsches Jungvolk* (German Young People) Boys aged 10–14
HJ = *Hitler Jugend* (Hitler Youth) Boys aged 14–18
JM = *Jungmädelbund* (League of Young Girls) Girls aged 10–14
BDM = *Bund Deutscher Mädel* (League of German Girls) Girls aged 14–18

In all four groups there was a great stress on political indoctrination, but in addition the sexes were moulded for their future roles in Nazi society. Boys engaged in endless physical and military-type activities and girls were prepared for their domestic and maternal tasks. In her memoirs, Melita Maschmann, a BDM leader, tried to put all this into perspective:

1 Apart from its beginings during the 'years of struggle', the Hitler Youth was not a youth movement at all: it became more and more the 'state youth organisation', that is to say, it became more and more institutionalised, and finally became the instrument used by
5 the National Socialist regime to run its ideological training of young people and the war work for certain age groups.

And yet the Hitler Youth was a youth organisation. Its members may have allowed themselves to be dressed in uniforms and regimented, but they were still young people and they
10 behaved like young people. Their characteristic surplus of energy and thirst for action found great scope in their programme of activities, which constantly required great feats to be performed. It was part of the method of the National Socialist Youth leadership to arrange almost everything in the form of competi-
15 tions . . . There were even story-telling competitions to see which boys and girls out of all their contemporaries were best at telling folk stories. This constant competition introduced an element of unrest and forced activity into the life of the groups even in peacetime. It did not merely channel young people's drive for
20 action: it also inflamed it, where it would have been wiser and better to give the individual within the group and the group as a whole periods when they could mature and develop in tranquility.

There was certainly a great deal of good and ambitious education in the Hitler Youth. There were groups who learned to
25 act in a masterly way. People told stories, danced and practised handicrafts, and in these fields the regimentation was fortunately often less strict. But the idea of a competition (behind which lay the glorification of the fighter and the heroic) often enough banished the element of meditation even from musical activities,
30 and the playful development of the creative imagination, free of any purpose, was sadly stunted.

* It is notoriously difficult to assess the success of any educational

All tools for the long term survival of the Nazi party (handwritten annotation)

system. Above all, it depends upon the criteria used for the assessment process, and even then, the mass of 'evidence' is open to conflicting interpretations. Historical conclusions about Nazi education are therefore of necessity tentative.

The teaching profession certainly felt its status to be under threat, despite its initial sympathy for the regime. The anti-academic ethos and the facile indoctrination alienated many, whilst the Party's preference for the HJ and its activities caused much resentment. Not surprisingly, standards in traditional academic subjects are generally agreed to have fallen by the early years of the war. Ironically, this was particularly the case in the various elite schools, where physical development predominated. The impact of the HJ seems to have been very mixed. In some respects the emphasis on team-work and extra-curricular activities was to be commended (especially when compared to the limited provision available in other European countries). However, the organisation suffered from its over-rapid expansion, which made for inadequate leadership in many areas, whilst the emphasis on military drill and discipline was certainly resented by many adolescents. It is all too easy to be taken in by the newsreel images of camaraderie and youthful exuberance for the cause. Much recent research suggests that German youth had not been won over by 1939, and that alienation and opposition to the regime increased markedly in the war years.

National Socialist Teachers League (handwritten annotation)

5 Religion

Germany is the home of the Protestant Reformation. It was the Saxon monk, Martin Luther, who destroyed the unity of the Catholic Church in the sixteenth century, and the subsequent religious divisions between Protestants and Catholics have persisted to this day. The rise of Nazism posed profound problems for the Christian Churches. How were they to respond to this powerful new phenomenon?

There can be little doubt that Nazism was based on a fundamentally anti-Christian philosophy. Although Hitler generally avoided direct attacks upon the Churches in the struggle for power, and Point 24 of the Party programme spoke in favour of 'positive Christianity' (an ambiguous phrase), it was impossible to hide the fact that the philosophies of Nazism and Christianity were mutually antagonistic. Christian ethics were the antithesis of Nazi values. Where Nazism glorified strength, violence and war, Christianity taught love, forgiveness and neighbourly respect. Moreover, on historical grounds Christianity was regarded as the product of an inferior race, and therefore it could not be reconciled with Nazi *völkisch* thought. Some leading Nazis, such as Himmler and his deputy, Heydrich, openly revealed their contempt. Hitler himself was more circumspect, although what were probably his true feelings were revealed in a private conversation in 1933:

[handwritten margin note: CELEBRATIONS IN CHURCH OF THE OPENING OF THE FIRST REICHSTAG]

1 Neither of the denominations – Catholic or Protestant, they are both the same – has any future left ... That won't stop me stamping out Christianity in Germany root and branch. One is either a Christian or a German. You can't be both.

To what extent were such attitudes borne out in practice during the 12 years of the Third Reich? To begin with the regime adopted a conciliatory stance towards the Churches. In his first speech as Chancellor, Hitler paid tribute to them as integral to the preservation of the nation. Members of the SA were encouraged to attend church services, in order to give weight to the idea that Nazism coincided with nationalist Protestantism. The 'Day of Potsdam' (see page 49) further gave the impression of a unity between the Protestant Church and the state. The Catholic Church likewise succumbed to the overtures of the Nazis. Frightened by the possibility of another *Kulturkampf* (the attack on it made by Bismarck in the 1870s), Catholic bishops were concerned to safeguard the position of the Church under the Nazis. In 1933 a Concordat was signed between the Papacy and the regime. In return for a commitment to keep out of all political activities, the Catholic Church was guaranteed religious freedom and its pastoral and educational roles were confirmed.

[handwritten margin note: RELIGIOUS INTERFERENCE DISREGARDED]

* However, the wooing of the Churches was totally insincere. They were merely being lulled into a false sense of security whilst the dictatorship was established. By the end of 1933 Nazi interference in religious affairs was causing resentment and disillusionment in both Catholic and Protestant Churches. The Catholic hierarchy soon discovered that the privileges promised by the Concordat were overtly disregarded: priests were harrassed and arrested; Catholic schools were interfered with; and secular organisations, such as youth groups, were undermined. In the Protestant Church *Gleichschaltung* was put into effect by the so-called *Deutsche Christen* (German Christians), who managed to reconcile their evangelical piety with Nazi ideas of national renewal. A new Church constitution was formulated in 1933 with the Nazi sympathiser, Ludwig Müller, as first Reich Bishop – an interesting application of the *Führerprinzip*. However, such Nazi successes alienated many Protestant pastors, and there soon developed an opposition group, the *Bekennende Kirche* (Confessing Church), which upheld orthodox Lutheranism and rejected Nazi distortions. Led by Pastor Niemöller, the Confessing Church gained the support of numerous pastors, and from 1934 it claimed to represent the true Lutheran Church of Germany.   *[handwritten note: bringing into line]*

By 1935 it was clear that the Nazi *Gleichschaltung* of the Churches had achieved only limited success. Yet the Nazi leadership remained torn between a policy of suppression, which could alienate large numbers of Germans, and a policy of limited persecution, which could allow the Churches an unacceptable degree of independence outside of state control. In fact, although the ultimate objective cannot be in doubt, from 1935 Nazi tactics degenerated into a kind of war of attrition against the Churches. A Ministry of Church Affairs was established and a broad range of anti-religious measures was implemented against both Churches: the abolition of denominational schools; campaigns of vilification against the clergy; administrative restrictions; and the arrest of more and more pastors and priests (Niemöller was interned in a concentration camp in 1938). The standing of the Churches was undoubtedly weakened by this approach, but it also stimulated individual declarations of opposition, including that of the Papacy itself, which vehemently attacked the Nazi system in *Mit Brennender Sorge* (With Burning Concern), its encyclical of 1937.

The outbreak of war initially brought about a more cautious policy, as the regime wished to avoid unnecessary tensions. However, following the easy military victories against Poland and France, and then the invasion of atheistic Russia, the persecution intensified. This was the result of pressure applied by anti-Christian zealots, such as Bormann and Heydrich, rather than the work of the weak and indecisive Minister of Church Affairs. Monasteries were closed, church property was attacked and church activities were severely restricted. Even so, Hitler did not allow subordination of the Churches to give way to wholesale suppression within Germany. It was only in the occupied territory of the Warthegau in Poland – the area designated as an experimental example of the 'New Order' – that events were allowed to run their logical course. Here, many of the clergy were executed, churches were closed down and the influenec of the Holy See was excluded. In the end the Nazi persecution of the Churches failed, but only because the war itself was lost.

In the place of Christianity the Nazis tried to cultivate a racial teutonic paganism, which became known as the German Faith Movement. Although never fully articulated, it revolved around four main themes: a wholesale rejection of Christian ethics; the propagation of the 'Blood and Soil' ideology; the exaltation of Hitler's personality; and the replacement of Christian ceremonies – marriage, baptism etc. – by pagan equivalents. Such neo-paganism never achieved support on any large scale (the 1939 census recorded 5 per cent of the population as members of the movement), but it represented another example of how the Nazi regime tried to undermine the established Churches.

The Nazis therefore achieved only limited success in their religious policy. As one historian has explained: 'The Churches were severely handicapped but not destroyed. Hitler's programme needed time: he was himself destroyed before it had taken root.' However, it has been maintained that the Christian Churches failed as well, in that their concern to uphold the institutions of Christianity was an abnegation of their moral duty actively to oppose a reprehensible regime. Why did they recoil from overt resistance, preferring accommodation with the

Nazis to self-sacrifice? The answer lies in the conservatism of both Churches. They distrusted the politics of the left which seemed to threaten the existing order of society and which in its most extreme form, atheistic communism, rejected the existence of religion itself. Equally though, there was a nationalist sympathy for Nazism, especially after the problems of 1918–33. It was all too easy to believe that Hitler's 'national renewal' was simply a return to the halcyon days before 1914. This was particularly true of the Protestant Church, which since the time of Luther had been closely aligned to the state apparatus. Finally, both Churches rightly feared the power of the Nazi state, and so a policy of heroic resistance was unlikely to achieve very much. In such a situation, concentration on pastoral and spiritual comfort was perhaps the most practical and realistic policy for the Churches.

6 Women and the Family

The first quarter of the twentieth century had witnessed profound sociological changes in German family life. Germany's demographic growth had decelerated markedly (which is not to say that the actual population had declined). In 1900 there had been over 2 million live births per annum, whereas by 1933 the figure was below 1 million. Over the same period female employment expanded by at least a third, far outstripping the percentage increase in population. Both of these trends had been partially brought about by long-term changes in social behaviour common to many industrialised countries. In particular, there was the recognition by many people that an improved standard of living would result from the use of contraception to limit family size, and the desire of a better educated female population to have a vocation as well as children. However, Germany's particular historical circumstances also exaggerated these developments. Economic mobilisation during the war had driven women into the factories, whilst post-war the difficulties caused by inflation had encouraged them to stay there out of economic necessity. In addition, the war had left a surplus of 1.8 million marriageable women, as well as many wives with invalided husbands. Finally, economic reorientation in the 1920s had led to an increased demand for non-manual labour, and the growth of mass-production techniques requiring more unskilled workers, both of which tended to favour the employment of women, who could be paid less than men.

The ideology of National Socialism was in stark contrast to these developments. It fundamentally opposed the social and economic emancipation of women. Indeed, Nazi anti-feminism has been described as 'a kind of secondary racism. The natural inferiority of women was an obvious if implicit corollary of the inferiority of non-Germans, non-Christians, non-Caucasians'. Such an interpretation would have been denied by the Nazis, who claimed to regard women as different rather than inferior. In their view, nature had ordained that the two sexes should fulfil entirely different roles, and it was simply the task of the Nazi state to maintain this distinction. What this amounted to in practice was that 'a woman's place was to be in the home'. Or, as the Nazi slogan presented it, a devotion to the three Ks – *'Kinder, Küche, Kirche'* ('children, kitchen and church'). Such dogma was upheld by the Party even before 1933 – there was not a single female Nazi deputy in the *Reichstag*, and a Party regulation of 1921 excluded women from all senior positions within its structure.

Nazi views on women tied in closely with their concern about the demographic trends. An expanding population was viewed as a sign of national strength and martial vigour – a reflection of Germany's aspiration to superpower status. How could they demand *Lebensraum* in eastern Europe, if the number of Germans was in fact levelling out? It was therefore considered essential to bring about a substantial increase in the population and to this end women were portrayed as primarily the mothers of the next generation – an image which suited Nazi anti-feminism. However, Nazi policy objectives for women and the family in no way reflected the social realities of twentieth-century Germany.

* To what extent were the Nazis able to reverse the prevailing trends? Initially attempts to reduce the number of women in work seem to have been quite successful. Between 1933 and 1936 married women were in turn debarred from jobs in medicine, law and the higher ranks of the civil service. Moreover, the number of female teachers and university students was reduced considerably. Such legislation obviously had a profound effect on professional middle-class women, although their actual number was small. In other sectors of the economy a mixture of Party pressure and financial inducements was employed to cajole women out of the work-place and back into the home. From June 1933 interest-free loans of 600RM were made available to young women who withdrew from the labour market in order to get married. The effects of the Depression also worked in the favour of Nazi objectives, since it not only drastically reduced the number of female workers (although proportionately far less than male workers), but it also enabled the government to justify its campaign for women to give up work for the benefit of unemployed men. On these grounds, labour exchanges and employers were advised to discriminate positively in favour of men. As a result of all this, although employment of women between 1932 and 1937 rose from 4.8 million to 5.9 million, it fell from 37 per cent to 31 per cent of the total.

The political arena was quite specifically excluded to women. The only opportunity available in this sphere was, as one historian neatly describes it, a 'surrogate emancipation' within the various Nazi women's organisations, like the NSF (*National Sozialistische Frauenschaft* – National Socialist Womanhood) and the DFW (*Deutsches*

Frauenwerk – German Women's Enterprise). Yet, the NSF and DFW were regarded by the Party as mere tools for the propagation of the anti-feminist ideology by means of cultural, educational and social programmes. And so when a campaign started in the NSF for enhanced opportunities for women within the Party its organisers were officially discredited.

However, by 1937 Nazi ideological convictions were already threatened by the pressures of economic necessity. The introduction of conscription and the rearmament declaration in 1935 soon led to an increasing shortage of labour, as the Nazi economy continued to grow. The anti-feminist ideology could only be upheld if economic growth was slowed down and that, in turn, would curtail the rearmament programme. This, of course, Hitler was not prepared to sanction. Consequently, market forces inevitably began to exploit this readily available pool of labour, and the relative decline in female employment was reversed. From 1937 to 1939, it rose from 5.9 million to 6.9 million, and from 31 per cent to 33 per cent of the total. In this situation the government even decided to end the arrangement whereby women who withdrew from the labour market would qualify for the marriage loan scheme.

The contradictions between theory and practice were exacerbated further with the onset of war. Germany's economic mobilisation was at first badly organised and not very efficient (see page 78). So, although there was no general conscription of female labour, the number of women at work continued to increase. In such a situation working women were the subject of considerable hardship. Long hours in an arms factory or the continuous demands of running a farm made life very arduous, especially if there were the added responsibilities of maintaining a household and raising children. Thus, when from 1943 Speer did try to mobilise the economy on a total war footing by suggesting the conscription of women workers, he encountered opposition from Bormann, Sauckel (the Plenipotentiary for Labour) and indeed from Hitler himself, who was always concerned about civilian morale. The Nazis were caught in the contradictions of their own ideology. In the final two years of the Nazi state more and more women ended up at work, and yet the government could not bring itself to renounce fully its anti-feminist rhetoric. An official in the NSF wrote: 'It has always been our chief article of faith that a woman's place is in the home – but since the whole of Germany is our home we must serve wherever we can best do so'.

Of course, the dilemma facing the Nazi state was made worse by its obsessive desire to increase Germany's population. This was encouraged in a number of ways: the enforcement of anti-abortion laws; the restriction of contraceptive advice and facilities; improved maternity benefits and family allowances; and the convertion of one-quarter of the marriage loan scheme into a straight gift from the state for each child born. Inevitably, this was all backed up by an extensive propaganda campaign, which glorified motherhood and the large family. There were also rewards: the Honour Cross of the German Mother in bronze, silver and gold, awarded for four, six and eight children respectively. Such glorification reached its sickening climax in the coining of the Nazi slogan 'I have donated a child to the Führer' (as contemporary humorists soon pointed out, this was presumably because of Hitler's personal unwillingness or inability to father children of his own).

Statistics do show quite clearly that from a low-point in 1933 the birth-rate did increase, reaching a peak in 1939, although thereafter it again slowly declined. The problem for the historian is deciding whether Nazi population policy was actually responsible for this demographic trend. Interpreting population statistics is notoriously difficult because it involves so many different factors – sociological, economic, and even personal psychological factors. Thus any mono-causal explanation is almost certain to be incorrect. Yet, trying to assess the *relative* significance of Nazi population policy against the import-ance of the end of the Depression, or the general trend to marry younger is fraught with problems. In this case, the cautious analysis, which merely accepts the interaction of these various causes, is more likely to be closer to historical reality.

One other significant factor of Nazi population policy was its aim not only to bring about a quantitative increase but also a qualitative improvement. Eugenic policy aimed to limit by sterilisation the reproduction of those people with hereditary diseases or anti-social behavioural problems such as alcoholism, and by 1939 375,000 such people had been forcibly sterilised. It also led to the establishment of one of the weirdest features of Nazi social engineering, *Lebensborn* (Spring of Life) – an institution which nominally cared for unmarried mothers of good racial credentials, but which also made the necessary arrangements for girls to be 'impregnated' by members of the SS.

Nazi views on women and the family were a natural concomitant to their rhetoric about the *Mittelstand*. As such, their ideological inten-tions were just as irreconcilable with the realities of twentieth-century Germany, and indeed clearly clashed with other Nazi objectives of rearmament and military conquest. Consequently, Nazi policy towards women and the family was contradictory and incoherent, and did little to affect the ongoing sociological trends of an industrialised society.

7 Cultural Life

During the evening of 10 May 1933 in the middle of a square just off *Unter den Linden* in Berlin there took place an event which soon became known as 'the burning of the books'. Thousands of tomes seized from private and public libraries were hurled into the flames by Nazi activists because they were considered undesirable on account of their Jewish, socialist or pacifist tendencies. For a nation whose literary heritage was perhaps greater than any other nation's in Europe, it was seen by many Germans and non-Germans alike as an act of mindless barbarism. It also rather aptly set the tone for the cultural life of Nazi Germany.

Culture was no longer to be encouraged according to the axiom of 'art for art's sake'. Rather, it was to serve the purpose of moulding public opinion, and with this in mind the Reich Chamber of Culture was supervised by the Propaganda Ministry. Germany's cultural life during the Third Reich was simply to be yet another means of achieving censorship and indoctrination, although Dr. Goebbels expressed it in more highfalutin language:

1 What we are aiming for is more than a revolt. Our historic mission is to transform the very spirit itself to the extent that people and things are brought into a new relationship with one another.

Culture was therefore 'co-ordinated' by means of the Reich Chamber of Culture, established in 1933, which made provision for seven sub-chambers: fine arts, music, the theatre, the press, radio, literature and films. In this way, just as anyone in the media had no option but to toe the Party line (see page 68), so all those involved in cultural activities had to be accountable for their creativity.

What kind of image did Goebbels hope to project and how was this achieved? Nazi culture was permeated by a number of key themes reflecting the usual ideological prejudices: anti-Semitism; militarism and the glorification of war; nationalism and the supremacy of the Aryan race; the cult of the Führer and the power of absolutism; anti-modernism and the theme of 'Blood and Soil'; neo-paganism and a repudiation of traditional Christian values.

The world of music managed to cope reasonably well in this environment, partly because of its less obvious political overtones and partly because of Germany's rich classical tradition, which was proudly exploited by the regime. However, Mahler and Mendelssohn, both great Jewish composers, were banned, as were most modern developments. The new wave of classical composers, Stravinsky, Schoenberg and Hindemith were disparaged and the new 'genres' of jazz and dance-band were respectively labelled 'negroid' and 'decadent'. Over 2,500 of Germany's literary community left their homeland during the years 1933–45. This fact alone is a sad reflection upon how such German writers and dramatists as Thomas Mann and Bertolt Brecht viewed the new cultural atmosphere. Their place was taken by a 'second XI', who either sympathised with the regime or accepted the curbs. It is difficult to identify a single book, play or poem written during the Third Reich, and officially blessed by the regime, which has stood the test of time.

'Comrades' by Arno Brecker

A There was once a nanny-goat who said,
   In my cradle someone sang to me:
   'A strong man is coming.
   He will set you free!'

   The ox looked at her askance.
   Then turning to the pig
   He said,
   'That will be the butcher'. (Bertolt Brecht)

B W. Beumelburg, *Gruppe Bosemüller*. In a trench in World War
   One Corporal Wammsch offers to send Private Siewers on
   leave following the latter's loss of nerve.

   'But I don't want to go away . . . I have to make up for
   something . . . give me time, why won't you give me some
   time? I don't want to go home, I don't want my leave . . . I
   don't want it . . . I want to go back to Fleury and the Souville
   ravine . . . that's all I want.'
   He is sobbing and shaking as if in a fever.
   Wammsch is terribly afraid. He hadn't expected this.
   'I don't want to go home . . . I'll go down on my knees before
   the captain . . . he will listen to me . . . I don't want to go home
   to my mother . . . I want to go to the Souville ravine and Fleury
   again.'
   Now he is exhausted at last. He is still sobbing and his whole
   body heaves. But he no longer resists. He calmly lets himself
   be taken into Wammsch's embrace, lets himself be carressed
   by Wammsch's hard hands, and there is something wonderful-
   ly dissolving in this feeling.
   'There . . .' says Wammsch, deeply moved, 'I'll go straight to
   the captain and talk to him. Of course you'll stay with us. The
   first one to give you an old-fashioned look is going to get my
   fist in his face . . .'

Actors, like the musicians, tended to content themselves with
productions of the classics – Schiller, Goethe (and Shakespeare) – in the
knowledge that such plays were politically acceptable and in the best
traditions of German theatre. The visual arts were also effectively
regimented by the Nazi constraints. Modern schools were held in total
contempt and Weimar's rich cultural awakening was rejected as
degenerate and symbolic of the moral and political decline of Germany
under a system of parliamentary democracy. Instead, encouragement

was given to works depicting the traditional Nazi themes in a mould of classical realism. As one historian has said: 'The best that can be said of the kind of painting and sculpture that was honoured by the Nazi movement was that it was no worse than the socialist realism in the Soviet Union'.

Only in the field of film can it be said that the Nazi regime made a genuine cultural contribution. Germany's cinematic reputation had been established in the 1920s, but continuity was maintained largely due to the fact that the major film studios were in the hands of nationalist sympathisers. Goebbels recognised the importance of this expanding form of entertainment and, on the whole, managed to reconcile political objectives with the integrity of the film-makers (only 96 out of 1,097 feature films produced between 1933 and 1945 were specifically at the request of the Propaganda Ministry). As a result, the talents of many 'Nazi' directors, such as Leni Riefenstahl, are still held in high regard by film buffs for their use of cinematic techniques to evoke great emotions despite the underlying political messages.

In the play *Schlageter* (1934) by Hanns Johst there is the line, 'whenever I hear the word culture, I reach for my gun'. It is a phrase which is often, and wrongly, attributed to Göring, but its acceptance by the Nazi authorities neatly underlines their philistine approach. Cultural life during the Third Reich was effectively muzzled – it could only operate within the Nazi strait-jacket and to that extent Goebbels succeeded. However, the regime most certainly failed in its attempts to create a Nazi cultural identity firmly rooted in the minds of the *Volk*. Some might suggest that it was simply a question of time, and that the regime's success in building new theatres and libraries and attracting more people to cultural events would have eventually brought about the desired result. On the other hand, the very powerful cultural resurgence throughout Germany since 1945 suggests that the traditions and spirit of Germany's cultural identity was too deeply imbued to be expunged by an essentially destructive and negative force such as Nazism.

8 A Social Revolution?

At first sight it might seem strange even to suggest that Germany underwent a 'social revolution' during the The Third Reich, for Nazism was a movement of the extreme right, and revolutions are normally associated with left-wing political parties. However, as academic interest in the social consequences of Nazism has grown since the 1960s, so there have developed two major theses which have supported the notion of Nazism's revolutionary impact upon German society.

In his book *Hitler's Social Revolution*, published in 1966, David Schoenbaum argued that Nazism was a powerful modernising force in

Painting by Diego Rivera, 1933

German society. His interpretation is a complex one founded on the differentiation between what he describes as 'objective' and 'interpreted' social reality. Thus, on the face of it, he accepted that the Third Reich witnessed many of the typical changes one associates with a developing industrial society ('objective social reality'). However, many of these changes were at odds with the backward-looking ideology of Nazism. This glaring contradiction was countered, he claims, by the Nazis successfully projecting an image of a society devoid of the traditional ties of class and status. Thus, Nazi society was regarded by the people as united like no other in recent German history, a society of opportunities for young and old, classes and masses, a society that was New Deal and good old days at the same time'. In effect, the idea of the *Volksgemeinschaft*, of a community of Germans working together regardless of background or role in society, was the reality of the Third Reich as perceived in the minds of its citizens ('interpreted social reality'). In this sense, at least, Schoenbaum suggests the Third Reich witnessed a fundamental change in social values and attitudes, which formed the basis of a revolutionary national consensus.

Another interpretation which has gained increasing currency of late is the idea of 'a revolution of destruction'. According to this view, the changes in Nazi society, whether objective or interpreted, were so limited, incoherent and lacking permanence that the idea of social revolution is without substance. Instead, the real revolution is seen to be in the destruction wrought by the effects of total war – wholesale military defeat and occupation, the break-up of a united Germany and its eventual political division, massive economic dislocation, and the demise of the social elites and vested interests which had dominated German life since the mid-nineteenth century. A veritable 'year zero'.

Such interpretations have found little favour with those historians who point to the realities of the prevailing class structure in the Third Reich. For Marxists schooled in the tradition of East German historiography, any idea of social revolution in Germany before the arrival of the liberating ideology of Soviet Communism and the creation of the Communist People's Republic (1949) is nonsense. In their view, Nazism was not social revolution, but social reaction of the worst kind, since it reinforced traditional class alignments and strengthened the position of the establishment elites, especially the powerful interests of the military and capitalism, at the expense of more popular institutions, such as trade unions.

Of all the disputes about the Third Reich, the 'social revolution' versus 'social reaction' is one of the most complex. The mere definition of terms such as 'reaction' and 'revolution' is very difficult, and often becomes the focus of argument in its own right. Likewise, Nazism itself defies straight forward analysis. It was a unique mixture of forces which reflected a broad and varied social make-up. Therefore, when one tears away the propaganda and asks 'what were the real social aims of the

Third Reich?' and 'did the Third Reich achieve those aims?', unfortunately the answers remain very murky. It is difficult to gauge the direct impact of Nazism – as opposed to the effects of other forces for change. Germany's history in the first half of the twentieth century is tumultuous and German society had been experiencing great changes in the 60 years before 1933. Nazism was in power for only 12 years and six of those were spent fighting the bloodiest war in human history. Can the historian draw a line between Nazism and the war as a catalyst for social change? Should he try to draw that line, when it could be argued that war was a natural feature of Nazism? These are the kinds of questions which make any analysis of the social impact of the Third Reich an extraordinarily complex task.

In spite of such problems of interpretation, it is difficult to see the Nazi movement in power as exerting a revolutionary impact. Elements of the Party which did support radical social change were silenced; the framework of the existing class structure was not altered; and the concept of the *Volksgemeinschaft* was little more than an effective propaganda ploy. Schoenbaum's thesis is not easily disproved, but equally his view of a revolutionary change in popular attitudes and outlook is exceedingly difficult to substantiate. However, past experience generally suggests that attempts to bring about fundamental changes in attitude are notoriously difficult to effect. In reality, Nazism could not reconcile its own rather confused social ideology with the ongoing pressures for change within a developing industrial society. These contradictions were further exaggerated by the requirements of political pragmatism once the Third Reich was set on its course of territorial expansion and ultimately war. Thus, despite Nazi rhetorical support for the *Mittelstand* and the peasantry, both groups came under enormous social and economic pressure, and instead it was the traditional elites which continued to dominate and prosper. Women were supposed to stay at home and have more children, but their role tended to suit the economic demands of the situation. The Christian Churches were expected to wither away, but they survived. Nazi culture was meant to establish new roots in the *Volk*, but it exerted little more than a negative censorious role. If there was a revolutionary core to Nazism, one might argue that it is to be found in the obsessive nature and implementation of its racial policy. Otherwise, it is difficult to escape the conclusion that there was no accelerated social transformation in Germany between 1933 and 1945.

However, such an interpretation is not incompatible with the view that a revolution in German society took place in the *wake* of the Third Reich. A simple comparison and contrast between the years 1933, 1945 and 1957 makes the point. The social changes in Germany between 1945 and 1957 were far more substantial than in the previous 12 years. Certainly, continuities prevailed – cultural traditions and social institutions, such as the family and the churches, do not break down overnight. However, the wholesale collapse of the Third Reich also brought to an end Prussian militarism and its social basis, the *Junker* landed aristocracy: it led to the political division of Germany and the creation of two states with very different social and economic conditions, both of which were the result of alien cultures and political philosophies in the form of Anglo-American and Soviet occupying forces. Perhaps, ironically, this was the real revolutionary legacy of Nazism.

Making notes on 'The Social Impact of the Third Reich'

This is a difficult chapter to study in a number of respects: some of the ideas and terminology – both those put forward by the Nazis and those

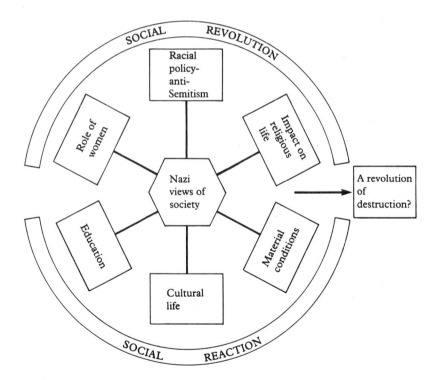

Summary – The Social Impact of the Third Reich

used by historians – are difficult to understand; and, although you need to go into a fair amount of detail with each section of the chapter, it is important that you do not become so swamped with 'facts' that you lose sight of the broader issues. Therefore, it would be a good idea to keep the following questions in mind *throughout*:

   i) What were the theoretical aims of Nazism for German society?
   ii) To what extent was the theory reflected in reality?
   iii) In what ways were Nazi theory and practice compatible and incompatible with each other?

However, it is probably easier to start by making your own notes following the structure of the chapter. You could then try to write some summarising answers to these questions. The following headings and sub-headings should help you:

1   **Nazi Views on Society**
1.1 The concept of the *Volksgemeinschaft*.
2   **Material Conditions**
2.1 Who lost? Who gained? And why? Workers; peasantry/farmers; *Mittelstand*; big business.
3   **Anti-Semitism**
3.1 Historical background.
3.2 The policy of gradualism.
3.3 The Holocaust.
3.4 Is it possible to explain rationally the Holocaust?
4   **Education**
4.1 Schools.
4.2 Youth movements.
4.3 Why is it so difficult to assess the impact of Nazism on educational provision?
5   **Religion**
5.1 Nazi policies on a) the Protestant Churches b) the Roman Catholic Church. Similarities and differences?
5.2 German Faith Movement. Did it have any religious significance or was it mere propagandist show?
5.3 In what ways did the Christian Churches reveal both their strengths and weaknesses during the Third Reich?
6   **Women and Family**
6.1 Historical background: population growth; changing status of women.
6.2 Work versus 'the three "K"'s'.
6.3 Population changes.
6.4 Did Nazism bring about any real change to population trends?
    Did Nazism bring about any real change to the role of women in society?
7   **Culture**
7.1 What did Nazi culture stand for?

Answering essay questions on 'The Social Impact of the Third Reich'

In this chapter you have looked at the social impact of the Third Reich in its broadest sense and hopefully you have begun to grapple with many of the issues raised. In preparing to answer essay questions on this topic it is vitally important that you are aware of the exact extent of your knowledge. Some questions will focus on a very specific area of content and will appear to be more straightforward. Others will be much broader in their coverage, but may be more analytically demanding. You must therefore be clear in your own mind that you have the necessary depth or breadth in terms of factual knowledge and analytical skills to answer any particular question. Study the following questions:

1 Why was Hitler able to make his own personal anti-Semitism such a powerful feature of German society?
2 Would you agree that the aim of creating a *Volksgemeinschaft* led to revolutionary changes in German society?
3 Compare and contrast the relationship of the Christian churches with the governments of Hitler and Stalin.
4 Did Nazi social and economic policies bring any benefit to the German people up to the outbreak of war?
5 'While man makes his supreme sacrifice on the field of battle woman fights her supreme battle for her nation when she gives life to her child'. To what extent was the Nazi view of women actually put into practice?
6 Examine the impact of the Third Reich on German cultural life.

With each question ask yourself what exactly is required for a good answer:
   a) Does it focus on one, several or all of the sections covered in this chapter?
   b) Does it need a knowledge of material from other chapters?
   c) Does it extend beyond Germany?
   d) What exactly are the chronological parameters of the question?

Many of the problems in examinations arise because students have planned their revision by trying to 'spot' questions in advance, and when the expected does not appear they find it difficult to escape from their own strait-jacket. For example, however much you might know about Nazism and religion, there is very little point trying to answer question 3 if you know nothing about the church in Stalin's Russia.

Of course it is not enough just to cover the correct factual material. You must also satisfy the analytical demands of the question. At first sight question 6 might appear the easiest and question 2 the hardest. But to gain high marks on question 6 you would have to go beyond a mere description of Nazi cultural policy. You would need to discuss at least the following four sub-questions:
a) What did Nazi culture stand for?
b) Was Nazi culture merely an extension of the propaganda machine?
c) How does the period of the Third Reich compare with earlier and later periods of German cultural history?
d) What is meant by the word 'culture'?

On the other hand, although question 2 appears daunting, you should be able to tackle it if you have digested the contents of this chapter well. Draw up a list of 5 sub-questions which will allow you to unlock question 2; re-order them with the intention of each sub-question forming the basis of a paragraph of the essay; and finally, write out a conclusion in full, making certain you get back to the fundamental issue of the original question.

Source based questions on 'The Social Impact of the Third Reich'

1 Anti-Semitism
Read the extracts from Maschmann, Himmler and Höss on pages 91, 92 and 93. Study the painting by Siwek on page 94.
a) In what ways do Maschmann's memoirs help to explain the development of anti-Semitism in Nazi Germany? (**3 marks**)
b) Höss's autobiography was written in gaol shortly before his execution. What characteristics does he display in the extract? (**3 marks**)
c) How do you explain the blunt and inhumane tone of Himmler's statement on this occasion? (**3 marks**)
d) Siwek's picture was painted in Auschwitz in 1943. What was the artist trying to communicate? Explain your answer in detail. (**5 marks**)
e) The Holocaust poses profound problems of interpretation for the historian. What are the problems of evaluation highlighted by these four sources? (**6 marks**)

2 Culture

Read the two written extracts by Brecht and Beumelburg on page 108. Study the two pieces of art on pages 107 and 110. Answer the following questions:
a) Which of the two written extracts was banned by the Nazi regime? Explain your answer fully by reference to both passages. (**6 marks**)
b) What was Brecker trying to communicate in his sculpture? (**4 marks**)
c) Explain fully why you think that Rivera's painting was not allowed to be exhibited in Germany until after 1945. (**4 marks**)
d) 'The historian can learn more about a society by studying what it has censored rather than what it has officially endorsed'. Do you agree? Explain your answer fully with reference to the above sources and other evidence known to you. (**6 marks**)

3 Education

Read the extracts on pages 95, 97 and 98. Answer the following questions:
a) According to the extract from the official of the National Socialist Teachers' League, what were the main aims of education in the Third Reich? (**3 marks**)
b) How far would you agree with the Nazi philosophy of History teaching? (**3 marks**)
c) Do you think that Maschmann provides an objective view of the Hitler Youth? Explain your answer. (**4 marks**)
d) What difficulties does the historian face in trying to assess the effectiveness of Nazi educational objectives? (**5 marks**)

CHAPTER 7

The Rise and Fall of the Third Reich

1 The Contours of Nazi Foreign Policy

Although this book is essentially concerned with the impact of Nazism upon the domestic history of Germany, the student of the Third Reich cannot ignore the issue of foreign policy and Germany's position in the international community. It would be wrong to treat domestic and foreign issues in isolation from each other, because, in the case of Nazi Germany, they are so clearly inter-related. However, it should be borne in mind that the coverage of the topic in this chapter is only partial and inevitably focuses on Germany's role (albeit a very important one) in events from 1933–45. For a more rounded discussion of international relations in the inter-war period it will be necessary to consult another volume in this series.

Despite the impositions and restraints of the Treaty of Versailles, and despite the dire economic condition of the country in 1933, Germany was able to pursue a major continental war within seven years of Hitler's assumption of power. This apparently remarkable transformation in her fortunes was largely made possible by the continental balance of power which had prevailed since 1918. The great empires of Russia, Austria-Hungary and Turkey had gone forever, creating a power vacuum in central and eastern Europe which could not be filled by a weak and isolated USSR, by the generally unstable successor states to the Habsburg empire, or by a modernising and inward-looking Turkish republic. Moreover, Britain and France had been decisively weakened by the effects of total war, whilst the USA had retreated into isolation and showed little inclination to uphold the European order which it had done so much to create in the years 1917 to 1919. In such a situation, the recovery of Germany with its vast economic potential and manpower, was always likely. Indeed, the revision of the Versailles settlement and the re-emergence of Germany as a great power had already begun under the Weimar Republic. What then were to be the aims of Nazi foreign policy?

In the decade after the Nuremberg trials of 1945–6 it was widely assumed that the expansionist aims of Nazi foreign policy dated from 1937. Hitler's address to the service chiefs and the Foreign Minister in November of that year, which was recorded in the so-called Hossbach Memorandum, seemed to mark the turning-point from a revisionist policy to one of aggressive expansion. Such a view is not now generally accepted.

As far back as 1960 the English historian Hugh Trevor-Roper, in his article *Hitler's War Aims*, drew attention to the systematic nature of Hitler's ideas on foreign policy from the very outset of his political career. Such an interpretation has been more fully developed by the so-called 'programme' school of historians (intentionalists) in Germany. In their view, Hitler had a clearly defined set of objectives, which amounted to a 'stage by stage plan' (*Stufenplan*). However, there remain conflicting opinions over the precise extent of his ambitions. The 'continentalists' believe that planned expansion was to be limited to the establishment of a hegemony within Europe: the 'globalists' go further and support the thesis that Hitler aspired to German supremacy in the Middle East and Africa (in particular, at the expense of British colonial territories) and finally to a struggle with the USA for world domination.

The 'programme' school has established an unusually high degree of acceptance within academic circles. Even the dispute between the 'globalists' and the 'continentalists' is rather contrived – since it does not revolve around what actually happened, but around the significance that can be accorded to some rather vague statements from Hitler himself on Germany's future world role. Yet, on essentials both interpretations are in agreement: they uphold the central place of Hitler himself in the creation of Nazi foreign policy; they emphasise the racialist framework of that foreign policy; and they view the conquest of *Lebensraum* as the basis upon which Hitler intended to build German status as a great power.

If many historians now accept the concept of some kind of Hitler 'programme', divisions of interprtetation do manifest themselves more obviously over the analysis of the actual events from 1933 to 1945. Whereas the 'intentionalists' maintain that Hitler's character and programme were the key factors in the shaping of German foreign policy, opponents in the 'structuralist' school have pinpointed other forces at work. In particular, supporters of the polycratic view of the Third Reich see all aspects of policy, including foreign policy, being shaped by numerous agencies and institutions, both inside and outside the Party. Some deny that there was any consistency. They see merely a confused variety of aims – 'expansion without object'. One historian even goes as far as to suggest that Hitler's goals were 'utopian' and that it was the dynamism of the Nazi movement, with its incessant demands for change which transformed *Lebensraum* from an 'ideological metaphor' into political reality. Another point of view relates the evolution of Nazi foreign policy to the domestic economic pressures building up in the second half of the 1930s. It is suggested that it was the need to overcome internal discontent created by the constraints of Nazi economic policy, which shaped Nazi foreign policy. In order to preserve his own political supremacy at home, Hitler was forced to accelerate his war-like ambitions.

Such attempts to portray Nazi foreign policy and strategy as the instruments of social forces have not threatened the established position of the 'programme' school. However, they do underline the need to be careful of imposing too much order and regularity on our historical explanations of Nazi foreign policy by utilising the benefits of hindsight. Secondly, they correctly draw attention to the dangers of Hitler-centred interpretations. The determining forces in any country's foreign policy are many. Even a dictator such as Hitler was not immune from circumstance and extra-personal factors. However, the ultimate direction of Nazi policy was undoubtedly a reflection of Hitler's personal ideological framework. In that sense, one can speak of *Hitler's foreign policy.*

2 The Revisionist Phase, 1933–7

a) The Beginnings of Nazi Foreign Policy

Hitler's appointment as Chancellor did not immediately usher in a new era in German Foreign Policy. Indeed, the post of foreign minister remained in the hands of Constantin von Neurath, a conservative Nationalist, which suggested continuity rather than change. Such a public perception suited Hitler. Economic and military circumstances demanded a cautious approach: Germany's unemployment had just peaked at 6.1 million and its army was still limited to 100,000 men. Moreover, the priority was the establishment of dictatorship at home rather than grandiose diplomatic escapades abroad. Consequently, in the early years of Nazi foreign policy, Hitler's objectives were limited to the cultivation of friendship with Britain and Italy to avoid Germany's isolation, and the weakening of French power and influence wherever possible.

Hitler was helped in this by the changing international situation, which was moving in Germany's favour. The Japanese invasion of Manchuria in 1931 had not only highlighted the ineffectiveness of the League of Nations, but had also underlined the strategic dilemma facing Britain: namely, how could it uphold the global commitments to its Empire, act as 'world policeman' for the League, and also play a major role in the defence of the European *status quo*. The severity of the Depression had already driven the USA further into isolation; whilst in France its effects, although felt later, were to contribute to the destabilisation of the political system and thereby pave the way for a lack of consistent resolve in foreign affairs.

However, the need for caution in this first phase of Nazi foreign policy was also effectively exploited, for it enabled the regime to appear to be reasonable and to lull many within Europe into a false sense of security. This was exemplified by Germany's withdrawal from the Disarmament Conference and the League of Nations in 1933, following France's refusal to accept parity in land forces. In this way it apeared as if the French were the unreasonable party, whilst Hitler had successfully evoked sympathy, especially from Britain and Italy (his two prospective allies). Similar benefits accrued from the unexpected signing of a 10-year non-aggression pact with Poland in January 1934. Not only did it create a favourable impression of reasonableness in international diplomatic circles, but it also falsely suggested to the Poles that an accommodation with Nazi Germany was possible. However, the pact's significance went further than mere propaganda; it effectively breached the French system of alliances in eastern Europe, and, in the short term, secured Germany's eastern flank while diplomatic problems were being dealt with in the south and west. In the long term, of course, Hitler did not envisage any place for an independent Poland – it served merely as the gateway to the creation of *Lebensraum* in the east.

Such successes did not result in any kind of formal agreement with Britain and Italy in the course of 1934. Although Britain showed considerable sympathy with Germany's revisionist demands, sympathy could not be equated with a military or strategic understanding, and several high level diplomatic missions failed to achieve any kind of breakthrough. An alliance with Italy also seemed a long way off. The attempted *coup* by Austrian Nazis in July 1934 probably enjoyed only moral support from Berlin, but it frightened Mussolini into deploying 40,000 troops to the Austro-Italian frontier, since he regarded Austria as a useful buffer-state, preferably under his influence. This incident was a clear indication of the limits of Nazi power at this time.

By the end of 1934 Hitler had secured his domestic position and the economy was recovering rapidly. His prestige was further enhanced in January 1935 when the Saarland, which for the last 15 years had been under the control of the League of Nations, voted in a free and fair plebiscite to return to German rule. It represented a great propaganda success for the Nazis. However, if Hitler was to loosen the shackles of Versailles unilaterally, it seemed that he would require greater military power than was permitted by the treaty. Therefore, it is a reflection of Hitler's great diplomatic skills that within two years the Versailles treaty was effectively dead and the continental balance of power had shifted in favour of Germany without a single shot being fired!

b) Breaking Free from Versailles

Germany's announcement in March 1935 of the existence of a *Luftwaffe*, followed shortly afterwards by the introduction of conscription and a peace-time army of 550,000, went directly against the terms of the Treaty of Versailles and led to a combined verbal condemnation by Britain, France and Italy – the so-called Stresa Declaration. Partly in response to Allied concern, Hitler spoke to the *Reichstag* about the futility of war just a few weeks later on 21 May:

1 The blood shed on the European continent in the course of the last 300 years bears no proportion to the national result of the

events . . . What dynastic egoism, political passion and patriotic
blindness have attained in the way of apparently far-reaching
5 political changes by shedding rivers of blood has, as regards
national feeling, done no more than touched the skin of the
nations . . . If these states had applied merely a fraction of their
sacrifices to wiser purposes the success would certainly have been
greater and more permanent.

It was in this uncertain international atmosphere that in June 1935
Britain and Germany signed a Naval Agreement which ignored the
terms of the Versailles treaty and allowed Germany to have a navy 35
per cent of the strength of the British fleet. Hitler had successfully
detached Britain from the Stresa Front and had laid the basis for a
fundamental Anglo-German understanding – or so he believed.

In the autumn of 1935 Mussolini ordered the invasion of Abyssinia
(also known as Ethiopia), one of the two remaining independent
African states. This destroyed the last vestiges of unity between Britain,
France and Italy. When it became clear that the aggressor was to be
allowed to triumph, it also underlined the impotence of the League of
Nations in major international incidents. Furthermore, it created an
atmosphere of crisis, which focused Anglo-French diplomacy on Italy
and on threats to the world order outside of Europe. In this situation
Hitler seized the initiative and ordered his troops to re-occupy the
de-militarised Rhineland in March 1936. It was a bold gamble which
did not enjoy the full support of the High Command or the Foreign
Ministry, who believed that the risk of military retaliation was too
great. Such pessimists were proved wrong and Hitler was proved right.
France showed no decisive inclination to intervene and Britain was
frankly indifferent. Condemnation was limited to verbal protests,more
directed at Hitler's methods than at his aims. With hindsight, it is clear
that the remilitarisation of the Rhineland was a decisive turning-point
in European international relations in the years 1933–9. In diplomatic
terms, not only the Versailles treaty but also the Locarno pacts had
been overturned. Most significantly, the strategic advantage of the
geographical and political buffer between France and Germany had
been lost completely. French military thinking had reflected the inertia
of its political leadership. It had been shown to be purely defensive and
clearly incapable of taking any kind of aggressive military initiative east
of the Maginot Line, the series of fortifications along France's border
with Germany.

In addition, Hitler's personal standing within Germany had been
enormously enhanced. One journalist later commented on the subsequent plebiscite on the remilitarisation:

1 99 per cent of the 45,453,691 registered voters went to the polls,
   and 98.8 per cent of them approved Hitler's action. Foreign

correspondents who visited the polling stations found some irregularities ... Nevertheless, this observer, who covered the
5 'election' from one corner of the Reich to the other, has no doubt that the vote of approval for Hitler's coup was overwhelming. And why not? The junking of Versailles and the appearance of German soldiers marching again into what was, after all, German territory were things that almost all Germans naturally approved.

The diplomatic pendulum continued to swing in Germany's favour during 1936. A civil war broke out in Spain. This caused further political uncertainty, which was exacerbated by the military intervention of Italy, Germany and Russia. Britain and France, fearing that the war could provide the spark for a major international conflict, struggled to maintain a policy of non-intervention. All this suited Hitler's purpose, for attention was again directed away from central Europe. It also provided a common focus for Italian and German interests which culminated in the emergence of the Rome-Berlin Axis in November 1936 – a *rapprochement* based upon political, economic and ideological co-operation, although not yet extending to a military alliance.

By the end of 1936 Germany's international status had undergone a remarkable transformation. France's previously dominant position on the continent had withered away and the diplomatic and military initiative had passed to Germany. The shackles of Versailles and Locarno had been struck off at no cost. Moreover, Germany was no longer isolated – Mussolini had been detached from France and Britain and was moving ever closer to an understanding with Hitler.

c) Plans for War?

However, Hitler's position was not without problems, especially since political and economic developments within Germany impinged so heavily on the evolution of his foreign policy (hence the danger of considering each in isolation). In the autumn of 1936 the economic crisis had revealed the fragility of Germany's economic expansion (see page 75). Hitler was not yet in a position to risk fighting a war; hence the establishment of the Four Year Plan under Göring to create a war economy. There was also the problem of conservative forces in the army and the foreign ministry. Certain elements in both these institutions had already advised a more cautious policy. If Hitler wished to raise the diplomatic stakes higher, he needed guaranteed support from such quarters. Finally, there remained the problem of securing an alliance with Britain. This had not materialised, and voices within the Party were promoting alternative diplomatic strategies. In particular, Ribbentrop, a leading and influential Nazi who operated his own personal 'bureau', was keen to develop a tripartite understanding between Germany, Japan and Italy at the expense of Britain. Hitler was not convinced, despite the developing cooperation between the three powers, and he remained wedded to the idea of the British alliance as a way of securing his long-term aim of crushing the USSR. Ironically, he sent Ribbentrop to London as Germany's new ambassador in the autumn of 1936 with the specified objective of securing an agreement with Britain.

It would seem that these problems provide a partial explanation of the relative inactivity of 1937, which clearly stands out as a dividing-line between the diplomatic coups of 1935–6 and the pre-war crises of 1938–9. However, in November 1937 at the so-called Hossbach Conference (named after Hitler's adjutant who took the surviving notes), Hitler addressed Foreign Minister Neurath, War Minister Blomberg and the three Commanders-in-Chief. The significance of the meeting has become the focus of considerable controversy. It was used by the prosecution at the Nuremberg trials and by some post-war historians to suggest that from this point 'the die was cast. Hitler had communicated his irrevocable decision to go to war'. At the other extreme it has been dismissed as simply a manoeuvre in domestic affairs to overcome the conservatives' doubts about the pace of rearmament. Hitler's ideas were 'in large part day-dreaming unrelated to what followed in real life . . . There was here no concrete plan, no directive for German policy in 1937 and 1938'. It is likely that the pressures of competing interest groups at home did prompt Hitler's statement and, certainly, events did not unfold as outlined in Hitler's scenarios – so the document does not provide a blue-print for Nazi foreign policy. However, it would be wrong simply to dismiss its contents out of hand, for it does show how Hitler's policy was changing from one centred on diplomatic initiatives to one where military force was to play a much greater part. Such a view is substantiated by two subsequent developments. Firstly, the re-structuring of the army's High Command and the appointment of Ribbentrop as Foreign Minister following further criticisms by Blomberg and Neurath about the dangers posed by the 'militarisation' of foreign policy: and secondly, the decision to develop an offensive war plan against Czechoslovakia.

3 The Road to War 1938–9

a) The Anschluss

Whatever doubts remain about the interpretation of the Hossbach Memorandum, it did make clear that Hitler's next objectives were to be Austria and Czechoslovakia. Austria's independence was guaranteed by the Versailles treaty. More practically, its position had been protected by Mussolini's desire to maintain a pro-Italian buffer on his northern frontier. However, by early 1938 the Austrian Nazi movement had re-established itself as a powerful and disruptive force following the failed *putsch* of 1934, while Mussolini's growing friendship with Hitler suggested that an accommodation over Austria would be possible. Hitler was hopeful that diplomatic pressure and internal disruption could bring about a peaceful *Anschluss*. When the Austrian Chancellor tried to counter such a possibility by organising a national referendum, Hitler was forced into a rushed and poorly-executed invasion of Austria in March 1938 (this was technically legitimised by a Nazi dictated 'invitation' given by the Austrian government).

The *Anschluss* with Austria represented a spectacular foreign policy triumph for Hitler, after a period of relative inactivity, although an interesting alternative perspective was provided by SOPADE, the SPD in exile:

1 In these reports we have often expressed the view that Hitler can count on the support of the majority of the people in two essential respects: (1) He has created work and (2) He has made Germany strong. The further the crisis recedes into the past the more the
5 first point will lose its attraction and the more the dictatorship will rely on support for its foreign policy line. The regime simply could not let slip such a favourable opportunity as the annexation of Austria for a general attempt to justify its policy.

Undoubtedly, the great majority of the German people was
10 prepared to approve the question posed in the plebiscite about the 'Reunification of Austria with the German Reich'. But the dictatorship cannot rest content with a majority, not even with a large majority. After the result of the last plebiscite was announced as 98.8 per cent, this time it could not be any less; it
15 had to be more. The dictatorship feels itself to be so weak that it could not bear it if it was only 97 per cent. Thus the dictatorship becomes a prisoner of its own methods.

In diplomatic terms the *Anschluss* had again shown Britain and France to be impotent or unwilling to stand up to Germany, whilst Mussolini had acquiesced to the loss of his Austrian buffer for the sake of German friendship. There were also economic advantages for the Third Reich – Austria's gold reserves and mineral deposits of iron-ore, copper and lead were of great value in the light of Germany's recurring balance of payment problems. Most importantly, Hitler had successfully overturned the strategic balance of power in central Europe. The western half of Czechoslovakia was now encircled, and control of the Danube valley from Vienna provided a gateway into south-eastern Europe.

b) Czechoslovakia

Having gained such a dramatic triumph over Austria, Hitler's attention

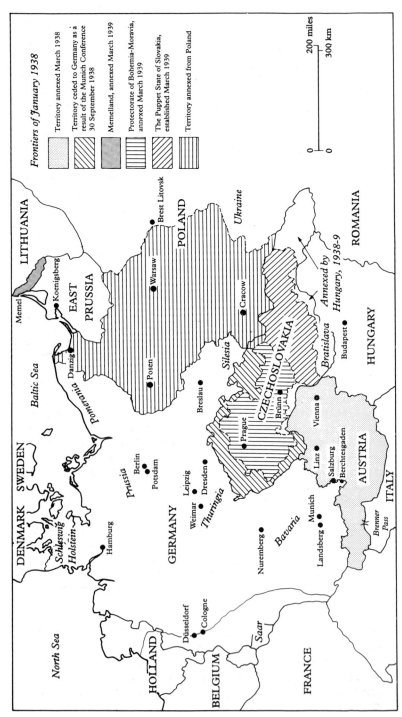

German Annexations 1938-9

turned almost immediately to the question of Czechoslovakia. The Czech crisis was to last almost a year and was to bring Europe very close to war. No clearer indication of Hitler's preparedness to use military force by this time can be found than his revised statement, written at the beginning of the military plan for the attack on the Czechs: 'it is my unalterable decision to smash Czechoslovakia by military action in the near future'. Of course, the existence of $3\frac{1}{2}$ million Sudeten Germans in the border region of Czechoslovakia, actively stirred up by the propaganda of the Nazi Sudeten German Party, provided the perfect method of undermining the Czech state from within. While the behaviour of Britain and France (despite the fact that the latter had a mutual assistance pact with Czechoslovakia dating from 1924) suggested that they would not interfere militarily in any territorial re-adjustments in the region. Hitler may not have been able to secure the desired alliance with Britain, but the diplomatic messages emanating from London convinced him that government there was prepared to write off Czechoslovakia for the sake of peace.

However, when the crisis came to a head in September 1938 – with constant clashes between Sudeten Germans and Czechs, with German and Czech troops poised on their respective frontiers and with the possibility of Britain and France being dragged into the war – Hitler settled for a diplomatic solution by accepting the Munich Agreement, which ceded only the Sudetenland to Germany. The whole incident was portrayed as another success for the Führer. Certainly, it completely cut the ground from under the feet of those generals who had been planning to arrest Hitler if war broke out. Yet, Hitler himself was far from pleased that his 'entry into Prague had been spoilt'. He had been aiming to destroy the Czech state in its entirety, but he backed down from a military invasion and accepted a negotiated settlement because he estimated that the risk of a more widespread continental war had become too great. There were also doubts about the nation's readiness for war. A government agency reported that:

1   There is no enthusiasm for military entanglements on account of the Sudeten German question. The uncertainty of the political situation is making the population depressed. Nobody wants to contemplate a war with England and France. The education of
5   the whole nation in the tasks required by a total war with all its burdens of various kinds is by no means adequate.
     The mood is in many cases depressed, mainly on account of the serious concern that sooner or later a war would put an end to the economic boom and would end in disaster for Germany.
10   In view of the diplomatic situation and the prospects for war which are often discussed without inhibition the mood can generally be described as depressed, serious and worried; there is a 'general war psychosis'.

The effects of the Munich Agreement were many and complex. For
Germany there were considerable economic and strategic advantages.
The Sudetenland was rich in natural deposits of coal, copper and
lignite; and it was also a strong manufacturing centre for textiles,
chemicals and machine tools. All these assets now passed to Germany.
Moreover, within the mountains of the Sudetenland, Czechoslovakia
had constructed its frontier defences. They too were simply taken over
by Germany, thus removing any real defensive capability from the
Czech state.

The crisis also had profound implications for European diplomacy
and the continental balance of power, since with hindsight it is clear
that Hitler was now prepared to pursue a policy of war, although he
wanted to fight any conflict on his terms. His ultimate objective was still
the creation of *Lebensraum* at the expense of the USSR, but hopefully
this could be facilitated by Britain's appeasement policy developing into
a more general acceptance of Germany's dominant position in central
and eastern Europe. As for the USSR, its exclusion from the decision-
making process at Munich was a clear sign of the failure of the
anti-fascist coalition which Stalin had tried to create under the banner
of the 'Popular Front'. Consequently, in the wake of the Sudeten crisis,
Soviet foreign policy began to re-align itself towards the possibility of
some sort of understanding with Nazi Germany which would be aimed
at preserving its own national security.

The last few months of peace witnessed frenzied diplomatic activity.
In March 1939 Germany had used diplomatic and military threats to
secure the self-dissolution of the Czech state (the provinces of Bohemia
and Moravia were annexed to Germany and Slovakia became a German
protectorate). Yet, although the western democracies did not respond
militarily to this overturning of the Munich Agreement, the Anglo-
French guarantee of Poland's independence two weeks later clearly
threw doubt on Hitler's hopes of a free hand in eastern Europe. Some
historians have pointed to the various military orders given at this time
for the establishment of long-range bomber squadrons and the construction of a large navy as symbolic of Hitler's 'internationalist'
ambitions and his preparedness to take on Britain. This may well be the
correct analysis of the long-term intention, but in the short term Hitler
most definitely did not want a war with Britain and France.

c) Poland

How could he avoid such a conflict while pursuing his claims against
Poland? In May 1939 he did manage to secure an alliance by the Pact of
Steel with Italy, but this was of limited military significance. It was the
hope of neutralising Britain and France which drove Hitler into the
arms of Stalin. Anglo-French negotiations with the USSR had made
limited progress and Stalin was becoming increasingly convinced that

the western democracies had no real sympathy for Soviet security concerns. This created a suitable atmosphere in which trade talks between Germany and the USSR could be re-established in July. Only a month later, a 10-year Nazi-Soviet Non-Aggression Pact was signed with additional secret clauses allowing for the division of eastern Europe into spheres of influence for the two powers.

Hitler was now confident that western military intervention would not follow a German invasion of Poland. Even while the negotiations were still taking place, Hitler told an assembly of senior commanders from the armed forces that there were no grounds for diplomatic or military doubts:

1 The enemy had another hope, that Russia would become our enemy after the conquest of Poland. The enemy did not reckon with my great strength of purpose. Our enemies are little worms. I saw them in Munich . . .

5   I shall give a propagandist reason for starting the war, no matter whether it is plausible or not. The victor will not be asked afterwards whether he told the truth or not. When starting and waging war it is not right that matters, but victory . . .

Close your hearts to pity. Act brutally. Eighty million people
10 must obtain what is their right. Their existence must be made secure. The strongest man is right.

Germany attacked her eastern neighbour on 1 September 1939 as planned. However, Britain and France stood by their guarantee to Poland, and two days later they declared war on Germany. Germany had become embroiled in a major continental conflict which involved military commitments on both its eastern and western fronts.

4   Why did the German Invasion of Poland Result in a Major European War in 1939?

By the end of 3 September 1939 Germany was at war not only with Poland, but also with Britain and France. Ironically, neither of these two countries, despite the popular backing for the declaration of war, had any real desire to take the military initiative against Germany, as was shown by the months of military inactivity which followed. So, how and why did Germany find itself in this unwanted situation?

It is hard to escape the conclusion that the fundamental cause lies with Hitler's grandiose foreign and racial policy. His desire for continental hegemony and the creation of *Lebensraum* at the expense of the USSR could only realistically be achieved (as he knew very well) by military force. In this sense the outbreak of some kind of war was implicit, as long as Hitler continued to direct German foreign policy, simply because he wished to overturn the existing *status quo* within

Europe (and perhaps beyond). This was clearly not acceptable to many other European countries. However, in 1939 Germany was certainly not economically or militarily prepared for a major continental war. Hitler only expected to fight a small-scale localised war against Poland, which would help to bolster Germany for the greater conflict to come. He was convinced (mainly as a result of advice from Ribbentrop) that the western democracies would not intervene, but in this analysis he was shown to be decisively wrong. Above all, Hitler failed to appreciate Britain's position. From the outset he had desired an alliance with Britain and, although this was clearly not a possibility by 1937, he continued to believe that under pressure some sort of reciprocal understanding was at least feasible. Undoubtedly, Chamberlain's own hostility to the USSR, combined with his readiness to pursue the policy of appeasement, contributed to Hitler's misapprehension. However, one of the traditional tenets of British foreign policy had long been to prevent one power dominating the continent of Europe. The annexation of Bohemia and Moravia convinced many in Britain that Germany under Hitler could no longer be trusted. Thus, despite Chamberlain's personal prevarications, attitudes in Britain towards Germany changed fundamentally and this made another 'Munich' in 1939 an impossibility. Britain and France guaranteed the independence of Poland in the hope of restraining Hitler and, although they were in a weak diplomatic position after the Nazi-Soviet Pact, they continued to stand by that guarantee. Consequently, when German forces did attack Poland, Britain and France – against the expectations of Hitler – actually did declare war on Germany.

5 Germany at War, 1939–45

Although Germany found itself committed to a major war in the autumn of 1939, which Hitler was not expecting to wage until the mid-1940s, it would be wrong to believe that Germany was militarily destined to fail from the start. The string of victories from September 1939 to November 1941 bear witness to the formidable military power exerted by the Nazi war-machine and suggest that Hitler could have extricated his country from the strategic quandary. The fact that he did not do this, so that by early 1943 Germany was facing almost certain defeat, has to be carefully explained and not merely assumed, as it is tempting to do with all the advantages of hindsight. Germany's eventual defeat was in no sense inevitable at the outset of the war.

a) Initial Victories, 1939–41

Poland's crushing defeat within a few weeks, endured without help from Britain or France, made available valuable raw materials and labour to supplement the aid already being received from the USSR according to the Nazi-Soviet Pact. Hitler was, therefore, keen to maintain the military momentum and planned for an invasion of France to take place as early as November 1939. The German attack was postponed several times, mainly because of the luke-warm attitude of senior army generals towards such an operation. It did not finally take place until May 1940, thus prolonging the Anglo-French 'Phoney War' for eight months. Hitler's thinking seems to have revolved around the idea of neutralising the western democracies before turning east again. To that end Germany needed 'to destroy France' and to reduce Britain to compliance with German aspirations on the continent. In this way it was hoped to force Britain under the pressure of military circumstances into an accommodation with Germany.

The German defeat of the Low Countries and France in six weeks was a dramatic triumph for both the armed forces and Hitler. Diffident generals could hardly fail to be impressed by the *Führer*'s military and political handling of events. German popular opinion was relieved and exultant. Hitler ruled not only in Berlin but also in Paris, Oslo, Vienna, Prague and Warsaw, while the Third Reich was bordered by the three 'friendly' powers of Spain, Italy and Russia. It was assumed by many that the war was as good as as over.

If common sense and a healthy self-interest had prevailed, Britain would have settled with Germany. But Churchill refused even to countenance negotiations. The implications of this stubbornness for Germany were clear-cut: Germany needed to secure air superiority, to invade Britain and to disable her military and strategic potential. Thus, Germany's failure to win the Battle of Britain in the autumn of 1940 was significant. But even more so was Hitler's personal decision to switch the military focus, and to start preparing for the invasion of Russia even before Britain had been neutralised. On 18 December 1940 Hitler issued Directive No. 21 for 'Operation Barbarossa', stating that 'The German armed forces must be prepared to crush Soviet Russia in a quick campaign even before the end of the war against England'. This decision can only be explained by Hitler's belief that *Blitzkrieg* tactics could also succeed in bringing a quick victory against the USSR, as they had against Poland, France and many others.

The invasion of Russia eventually took place in June 1941, having been delayed by the need to secure Germany's southern flank in the Balkans, where Yugoslavia and Greece (the latter following a failed Italian invasion) had sided with Britain. At first all went well. Vast tracts of territory were occupied and hundreds of thousands of prisoners were taken. Yet the Russians never lost the will to carry on fighting, and by December 1941 differences over military objectives between Hitler and his generals, Anglo-American aid and the snows of Russia had combined to bring the German advance to a halt. Hitler's gamble to break Russia by launching a *Blitzkrieg* invasion had failed and Germany was now committed to the prospect of a long war on two fronts.

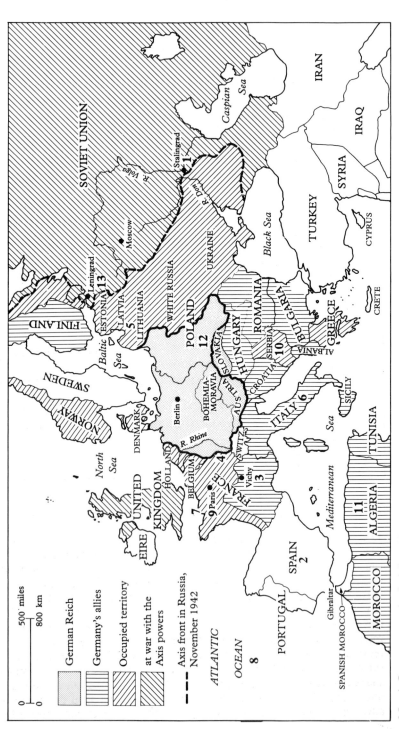

Nazi Germany at its height, 1942

Nazi Germany at its Zenith, 1942. See map on facing page

1 Stalingrad. German surrender, January 1943. Turning-point on the eastern front.
2 Spain. Civil war, 1936–9. Despite the victory of Franco's Nationalists and the military aid given by Nazi Germany, Spain remained neutral.
3 Vichy. Capital of collaborationist French regime under Marshall Petain.
4 Maginot Line. French defensive line of fortifications along Franco-German border.
5 Baltic states. Estonia, Latvia, and Lithuania. Annexed by USSR under the terms of Nazi-Soviet Pact. Occupied by German forces from 1941–4.
6 Italy. Germany's ally, 1940–3. Northern half of peninsula occupied by German forces following overthrow of Mussolini.
7 Normandy. Allied landings, June 1944 (D-Day).
8 Battle of the Atlantic. German U-boat campaign failed to stop Allied convoys, 1941–3.
9 Paris. Paris and northern France occupied by German forces, June 1940–August 1944.
10 Serbia. Partisans under leadership of Tito resist German occupation.
11 French N. African colonies. Morocco, Algeria, Tunisia. Under control of Vichy France. German troops ejected by Allies, May 1943.
12 Auschwitz. Largest extermination camp.
13 Leningrad. 900-day siege.

b) The Turning of the Tide, December 1941–January 1943

December 1941 was a turning-point in another sense too, for the Japanese attack on the USA's naval base at Pearl Harbor 'globalised' the conflict. Although he was not obliged to do so, Hitler aligned Germany with Japan and declared war on the USA. This move was perhaps prompted by America's involvement in the Battle of the Atlantic even before Pearl Harbour. However, it did not fit easily with Germany's existing strategy and above all it turned the industrial capacity of the world's greatest power against his own country. It is tempting therefore to suggest that by the end of 1941 Hitler was losing the military and diplomatic grasp which had previously allowed him to shape international developments. Events were now very much running out of the *Führer's* control. He was beginning to respond to circumstances and to make strategic judgements which were largely shaped by his own capacity for self-delusion and by his own warped view of the world, rather than by any rational assessment of situations.

Although, with hindsight it appears that the decisions made by Hitler in December 1941 were indeed the vital turning-point for German fortunes in the war, this was certainly not apparent at the time. Throughout 1942 German forces pushed deep into the Caucasian oilfields with the objective of capturing Stalingrad, while the Afrika Korps drove the British back across North Africa into Egypt. It was the failure of these two offensives which enabled contemporaries to see the winter of 1942–3 as 'the turning of the tide': the British victory at El Alamein (November 1942) eventually led to the ejection of German forces from North Africa; and the encirclement and surrender of 300,000 troops at Stalingrad marked the beginning of the Russian counter-offensive. The implications of the situation were difficult to hide from the German public:

1 How different the atmosphere is from that of the first war year when at the slightest provocation red Nazi flags were flown, drums were beaten on the radio announcing victory. Since the defeat at Stalingrad and the realisation of total war, all is grey and
5 still and on 14 August [1943] Goebbels declared total war to all at home. Everyone was called up, even women up to 50 years old, and mere boys had to do anti-aircraft duties.

c) Defeat

From 1943 Germany's stategy was essentially defensive. Hitler was determined to protect 'Fortress Europe' from allied invasion, but his strategic and political thinking was losing touch with reality. Increasingly it was shaped solely by belief in German invincibility and his own ideological prejudices about race and communism. For, in spite of all the military difficulties, the creation of the new racial order continued – there was no postponement of the programme to exterminate the Jews. Hitler deluded himself into thinking that the alliance of the USSR and the western allies could not last and that this would then allow Germany to play off one against the other. However, allied military co-ordination continued to work reasonably well. By the end of 1943 Anglo-American forces had linked up in Africa and had then established a hold on Southern Italy, while Russian forces, in the wake of the great tank victory at Kursk, had reconquered much of the Ukraine. The war had also begun to have an impact on Germany itself. The massive bombing raids wreaked destruction and dislocation, although their exact strategic value has been seriously questioned in recent years. It was becoming clear the war could not be won and that Germany faced total devastation unless the allied demand for 'unconditional surrender' was conceded. Such realities prompted the attempted assassination of Hitler (see page 72) in July 1944. Its failure meant that the war would have to be fought to the bitter end. Thus, strong German resistance forced the western allies to fight extremely hard in order to break out of the beach-head established in Normandy in 1944, whilst in the east the Russian advance ground remorselessly through eastern Europe in the face of desperate defensive measures. Yet, a blind optimism still prevailed in the minds of some, as Albert Speer, the Minister for Armaments and a close friend of Hitler, later explained:

> 1 In Westphalia a flat tyre forced us to stop. Unrecognised in the twilight I stood in a farm-yard talking to farmers. To my surprise, the faith in Hitler which had been hammered into their minds all these last years was still strong. Hitler could never lose the war,
> 5 they declared. 'The Führer is still holding something in reserve that he'll play at the last moment. Then the turning-point will come. It's only a trap, his letting the enemy come so far into our country'.

It was not until April 1945, when Russian soldiers had advanced to within a mile of the Chancellery in Berlin, that Hitler committed suicide. Only then was the German nation freed from the *Führer*'s grip and only then could the war end.

6 Conclusion

By May 1945 Germany lay in ruins. Nazi foreign policy had reached its destructive and nihilistic conclusion. Its ambitions had been grandiose: to establish a 'greater Germany', which went well beyond the Bismarckian legacy of 1870; to destroy Bolshevik Russia; and to create a new (world?) order based on the concept of the racial supremacy of the Aryan. Moreover, the means to these ends had also involved the willing acceptance of violence and bloodshed on a massive scale. Yet, it would be incorrect to suggest that German foreign policy had undergone an about-turn in 1933. Expansionism clearly stands out as a thread of continuity in German history from the time of the *Kaiserreich* onwards. The unexpected failure of Germany to achieve its ambitions in the First World War left a legacy of unrequited aspirations at many levels of German society, which were strengtheneded by the *Diktat* of Versailles. All Weimar governments were committed to fundamental revision of the Versailles treaty, whilst throughout the 1920s powerful voices in the armed forces continued to advance more radical proposals to restore Germany's continental position.

The development of Nazi foreign policy must, therefore, be viewed in the light of such traditions and circumstances. Hitler advanced ideas sufficiently similar to those of the conservative elites in the army, foreign ministry and big business for them to gain general acceptance among the established ruling circles in Germany. However, this is not to suggest that Hitler was a mere 'agent' of other social forces. Nor does it imply that there was a clear-cut consensus about the direction of German foreign policy in Party and state. The fact that alternative points of view and strategies continued to exist reflects the rather confused structure of government in the Third Reich. Nevertheless, it is clear that in spite of all the political pressures and demands, the ultimate direction taken by Nazi foreign policy was a reflection of Hitler's personal ideological framework and strategy. In that sense it remains valid to speak of Hitler's foreign policy and Hitler's war.

That Hitler failed in his ambitions can be explained on a superficial level by his strategic bungling. Hitler had always believed (shaped largely by his own personal experiences as a soldier) that a war on two fronts had to be avoided. To this end he needed an alliance with Britain – or at least its benevolent neutrality – so that he could launch an unrestrained attack in the east. Consequently, when Germany failed to secure either British neutrality or a British surrender in 1940–1, before attacking the USSR, the long-term cause of defeat was laid. Germany had become engaged in a conflict for which it was not fully prepared, and therefore resources and economic power were once again stretched beyond the limits of military logistics. The alliance with Mussolini's Italy was no substitute. Indeed, Italian military weakness in the Balkans and North Africa proved costly, since it diverted German forces away from the main European fronts. Yet, Hitler was driven on obsessively to launch the ideological crusade against Russia. The failure to defeat Russia by the onset of winter, combined with the entry of the USA, now tipped the balance. Britain was still free to act as a launch-pad for a western front and in the meantime could strike into the heart of Germany by means of aerial bombimg. Russia could maintain the eastern front relying on its geography and huge manpower. Above all, however, the resources and industrial capacity of the world's two industrial giants were now directed towards the miltary defeat of Germany.

Such an interpretation might give the impression that historical explanation can be a relatively straightforward exercise. It seems so logical and clear-cut. However, before accepting such a mechanical view of Germany's defeat in the Second World War, it should be borne in mind that even in 1942 Germany came very close indeed to capturing Stalingrad and to defeating Britain in Egypt. Such successes would have changed the course of the war with unpredictable results.

Making notes on 'The Rise and Fall of the Third Reich'

It is vital to remember that this chapter can serve only as a starting-

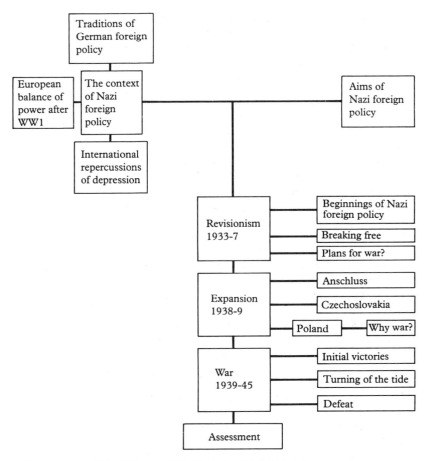

Summary – The Rise and Fall of the Third Reich

point for your study of this topic. You will be able to understand and appreciate the finer points of the debate, only if you have gained a broader perspective by i) finding out about the development of German foreign policy from 1918, and preferably from 1890; and, ii) considering German foreign policy in the broader context of international relations from 1918 to 1945.

Those of you following outline courses will probably already have done some work on the first issue. If you have, now might be a good time to refresh your memory about what you have studied previously. Some of you will also have started to build up a picture of the second issue when considering the history of other states. Again, now would be a good time to look back at some of the notes you made then. However, if you want to gain a good general analytical overview of both issues, the most effective way would be to study one of the books on international relations in this series.

Following the reading of this chapter there are two important tasks to carry out:

1 Construct two chronological tables – one for the period 1933–9 and one for the period 1939–45. In each case divide your sheet of paper into three columns with the following three headings:
   a) Major domestic events in Germany
   b) Initiatives in German foreign policy
   c) International developments
   It might be a good idea to refer to the Chronological Table on pages 150–151 to assist you with this task.

2 You need to begin to grapple with some of the important issues raised about German foreign policy. Therefore, you should try to write summarising answers to the following questions:
   a) What exactly were the foreign policy objectives of Hitler?
   b) To what extent did Hitler's methods of handling foreign policy change over time?
   c) Why is it dangerous to differentiate between Nazi domestic and foreign policies?
   d) Why did war break out in September 1939?
   e) Why did Germany suffer such a cataclysmic defeat in the war?

Answering essay questions on 'The Rise and Fall of the Third Reich'

There is a whole range of possible questions on this topic, though on the whole examiners tend to favour the general question which requires a broad analytical overview. A popular way to pose such general questions is to take a quotation from an eminent historian and then invite you to 'discuss'. Study the following examples:

1 'Consistency of aim with complete opportunism in method and tactics.' (Bullock) Discuss this assessment of Hitler's foreign policy.
2 'Hitler did not make plans – for world conquest or for anything else. He assumed that others would provide opportunities, and that he would seize them.' (Taylor) Discuss.
3 'The ultimate objective of Hitler's programme was undoubtedly revolutionary.' (Hildebrand) Discuss.
4 'The similarity in the directions, even if not in the essence of German aims in the two world wars is striking.' (Fischer) Discuss.

Too often students are fooled by the use of a well-known historical name into trying to prove the assertion made in the quotation used. However, the key word is 'discuss'. With each question you must draw up a list of factors to support the quote and a list of factors to counter it. You must do this, even if your first reaction is to agree with the initial assertion. It is vital that you examine both sides of the debate.

Choose one of the above questions and prepare a detailed essay plan by carrying out the following tasks:

a) Make a list of points for each side of the argument, so that each one can form the basis for an individual paragraph.
b) Briefly note down relevant supporting details and examples against each point.
c) Write a short concluding sentence for each intended paragraph – making certain to refer back to the ideas that lie behind the quotation.
d) Write out in full a conclusion for the whole essay. Be sure to focus very specifically on the wording of the quotation and to make some sort of overall judgement. For example:
  i)   Totally agree or disagree, but say why you are so certain.
  ii) Essentially agree or disagree, but recognise that it is important not to forget the significance of other factor(s).
  iii) Cannot decide – the evidence is not clear-cut. Therefore you must conclude that the quotation oversimplifies a more complex situation.

Source-based questions on 'The Rise and Fall of the Third Reich'

1 Hitler's Attitude to War
Study the two extracts from Hitler's speeches on pages 121–2 and 129. Answer the following questions:
a) Explain 'I saw them in Munich' (page 129 line 4). (**1 mark**)
b) Comment on the contrast in tone and language between the two extracts. (**3 marks**)
c) How do you explain the differences between the two extracts? (**4 marks**)
d) Explain in your own words how Hitler assessed Allied diplomacy in 1939. Do you think that his assessment was accurate? (**5 marks**)
e) 'The war of 1939 was far from premeditated. It was an avoidable mistake.' How far do these sources and other evidence known to you support this assertion? (**7 marks**)

2 Public Opinion and Foreign Affairs, 1936–9
Study the three extracts commenting on public opinion on pages 122–3, 125 and 127. Answer the following questions.
a) Explain i) 'the Sudeten German question' (page 127 line 2), and ii) 'the junking of Versailles' (page 123 line 7). (**4 marks**)
b) How do the authors of the first two extracts explain the high percentage of votes cast in favour of Hitler's regime in the plebiscites? Refer to similarities and differences. (**6 marks**)
c) How do you explain the conclusion reached by the third extract? (**4 marks**)
d) What problems do these extracts highlight about the assessment of public opinion under a dictatorship? (**6 marks**)

3 Popular Attitudes to the War
Study the two extracts on pages 134 and 135. Answer the following questions.
a) Explain i) 'total war' (page 134 line 5), and ii) 'defeat at Stalingrad' (page 134 line 4). (**2 marks**)
b) What might be the reasons for the contrast in public expectation described in the two extracts? (**4 marks**)
c) The first extract is from a private diary and the second is from a book written in 1970 by a leading figure in the Third Reich. In what ways would this affect a historian's assessment of the extracts' reliability as evidence of popular attitudes towards the war? (**4 marks**)

CHAPTER 8

Conclusion: The Third Reich and German History

From the outset, the emergence of the Nazi regime presented observers not only with profound political and economic questions but also with serious moral issues to resolve. For example, most left-wing and liberal intellectuals saw Nazism as an essentially evil (and therefore morally reprehensible) movement. This moral dimension has not diminished with the passage of time, even though Nazism is now an historical issue. Indeed, with the revelations of the full extent of the Nazi horror in 1944–5 and the still regular news of 'war criminals' and 'war crimes', it is almost impossible not to explain the rise of Nazism without giving consideration to its moral implications. Thus even the seemingly most objective of historical questions are likely to be answered with more than a small amount of subjectivity.

Why did the German people reject democracy? Why did one of the most advanced and civilised nations in Europe witness the growth of such a brutal political movement? Why was that movement able to become and remain the legitimate government of Germany? Such questions have been at the heart of the debate on Nazism since the 1930s. The modern student is therefore already faced with a wide variety of possible answers and historical interpretations, and these continue to be added to as new evidence becomes available and as new generations view events with different perspectives.

1 Contemporary Views

In the 1930s left-wing analysts faced considerable difficulties in their attempts to explain the rise of Nazism (and by extension of fascism in general), since Marxist dialectics had made no provision for the development of such a movement. Eventually, at the Seventh Congress of the Communist International in 1935, fascism was defined as 'the open terroristic dictatorship of the most reactionary, most chauvinistic and most imperialist elements of finance capital'. And this in fact remained the ideological basis of East German and Soviet scholarship on Nazism until the unification of the two Germanies in 1990. Stripped of its verbiage, the theory proposes a close connection between Nazism and capitalism. More particularly, it views the Nazis as mere agents for the string-pulling capitalists, who, in order to satisfy their imperialist ambitions and their desire for profits, dominated a powerful political movement so as to suppress the revolutionary workers. According to such a Marxist interpretation, therefore, fascism was the last stage of capitalism, which would soon collapse because of its own internal contradictions and would thus usher in the age of socialism.

The difficulty with any 'generic' explanation of the rise of European fascism is to substantiate it convincingly with historical detail in particular cases. With Germany in the 1930s the evidence is unconvincing. Contacts did exist between Nazism and big business, and the Nazis did receive financial backing (see page 24) from many major industrialists. However, it is difficult to substantiate the claim that the Nazis were merely the agents in this group. 'The "agent theory" is unable to expose the transmission belts between the monopoly capitalists and their agents' (M Kitchen). Moreover, in their attempt to explain fascism in economic terms, Marxist analysts neglected important political aspects. Greater emphasis on the 37 per cent of the population who actually voted for Hitler in 1932 would surely have persuaded the Communist International that National Socialism was something more than a movement of financial capitalists at a time of economic crisis.

However, left-wing arguments about the historical inevitability of Nazism were matched by some equally unquestioning views in more conservative circles. When Britain found itself at war with Germany again in 1939 some strong opinions were expressed about the reasons behind the emergence of Hitler's regime. In 1941 Sir Robert Vansittart, Chief Diplomatic Adviser, gave a series of radio broadcasts entitled 'Black Record – Germans Past and Present'. He upheld the view that 'Germany as a whole has always been hostile and unsuited to democracy', and claimed that Hitler's dictatorship had evolved from the authoritarian system of Bismarck and the Kaiser: 'No other race could have managed to idolise such people.'

Vansittart's views can be put down to his long-standing anti-German feelings and to the requirements of war-time propaganda. However, even some academic historians of the 1940s followed a similar line of thought. One of them wrote in a book published in 1941 on the roots of National Socialism:

> National socialist theory is almost entirely derived from the common elements in traditional German thought during the past 150 years. For that line of thought, which leads from Herder to Hitler, is traditionally and typically German.

Even the renowned A.J.P. Taylor expressed similar opinions in *The Course of German History* in 1945:

> 1 It [the Third Reich] was a system founded on terror, unworkable without the secret police and the concentration camp; but it was also a system which represented the deepest wishes of the German people. In fact it was the only system of government ever created
> 5 by German initiative . . . it rested solely on German force and German impulse; it owed nothing to alien forces.

Not surprisingly, such views were not uncommon in those countries at war with the Third Reich in the early 1940s.

2 Post-War Interpretations

In the years immediately after the Second World War two major lines of interpretation prevailed. There were those non-German historians who continued to argue in much the same vein as Vansittart had done. The culmination of this view was probably reached with the publication in 1959 of William Shirer's *Rise and Fall of the Third Reich*. This monumental work, written by an American journalist who had worked as a correspondent in Germany between 1926 and 1941, made a profound impact on the general public. In it he explained how Nazism was 'but a logical continuation of German history'. He argued that Germany's political evolution, its cultural and intellectual heritage and the people's national character were all contributory factors in providing German historical development with an inner logic which led inevitably to the success of Hitler and the creation of the Third Reich.

Not surprisingly, the implicit anti-German sentiments of historians from Allied countries were not kindly received in Germany, especially amongst those intellectuals who had in fact opposed Hitler. As a consequence, there emerged in the post-war decade in West Germany a school of thought which emphasised the 'moral crisis of European society'. It was epitomised above all by the writings of G. Ritter who focused on the European circumstances in which Nazism had emerged. In his view, it was hard to believe that Germany's great political traditions, such as the power of the Prussian state, or its rich cultural history could have contributed to the emergence of Hitler. Instead, Ritter emphasised the events and developments since 1914 in Europe as a whole. It was the shock given to the traditional European order by the First World War which created the appropriate environment for the emergence of Nazism: the decline in religion and the traditional standards of morality; a tendency towards corruption and materialism; above all, it was the emergence of mass democracy at such a time, which a cynical demagogue like Hitler could exploit for the satisfaction of his own ends.

The 1960s witnessed the beginnings of a phenomenal growth in academic literature on the Third Reich. This was partly due to the fact that the German archives in the hands of the Western Allies were made available, but it was also a result of the major controversy generated by the publication of a book ironically not even on the subject of Nazi Germany. Fritz Fischer's *Griff nach der Weltmacht* (Germany's Aims in the First World War), first published in Germany in 1961, shattered the easy calm within West German historical circles. Its major thesis was that Germany's objectives in July 1914 had undoubtedly been offensive and had been intended to establish Germany's hegemony over continental Europe. The implications of this thesis were profound, for it clearly suggested a similarity between the foreign policy aims of the *Kaiserreich* and the Third Reich, which in turn upheld the idea of a continuity in development between the two regimes. However, it was not only Fischer's message but also his method of delivery which was so significant. Fischer in effect ushered in the start of a methodological revolution in historical research. His interpretation was based upon an analysis of the interaction between Imperial domestic and foreign policies, and in particular on the role of the traditional elites in German society. In this way, Fischer laid the basis for the emergence of the 'structuralist' school.

Since the late 1960s 'structuralist' historians have exerted an enormous influence on our understanding of the Third Reich (although they have paid even more attention to the *Kaiserreich*). Without resorting to the crudities of historical determinism, they have debunked the notion that Nazism was an 'accident' divorced from Germany's historical development. Instead, they have drawn attention to its continuities with the past: the existence and influence of conservative social elites, especially in the armed forces and the bureaucracy; and the prevalent belief that Germany deserved as of right the status and territory due to a great power. Above all, they have emphasised the complexities of the Third Reich as a power structure by highlighting the limits of Hitler's leadership and forward-planning. Furthermore, by focusing on the role played by other institutions and social groups in the Third Reich they have underlined the element of continuity provided by Germany's social elites.

However, the 'intentionalists', the conservative opponents of the 'structuralist' interpretation, have continued to maintain a strong rear-guard action. For many of them Nazism can be directly equated with Hitlerism, and there is no escape from the central importance of Hitler the individual in the Nazi seizure of power and the regime that followed. Even so, it is important to realise that the analysis provided by the 'intentionalists', while considering the personality and ideology of Hitler to be essential, goes well beyond the framework of mere biography. This, in essence, is the stance taken by Germany's leading historian of Nazism since the 1960s, Karl Dietrich Bracher. Bracher upholds the fundamental role of Hitler, and accepts the term Hitlerism as a direct alternative to Nazism. However, as implied by the title of his most famous book, *The German Dictatorship*, published in 1970, he also sees Nazism as a uniquely German/Austrian phenomenon. It arose in a society shaped by the nineteenth century 'German problem' and then devastated by war and humiliated by defeat. It succeeded in gaining power because of Hitler's own powerful nationalist ideology and because his policy of legality confused nearly all the opponents of the Nazis until it was too late:

1 Hitler's road to power was never inevitable, since rarely in history
  has there been such a close inter-dependence of general and
  personal factors and the indispensable role of the individual as in
  the crucial period between 1919 and 1945, from Hitler's entry
5 into politics to his exit . . . It was indeed Hitler's *Weltanschauung*
  and nothing else that mattered in the end, as is seen from the
  terrible consequences of his racist anti-semitism in the planned
  murder of the Jews.

The most recent development in the historiography of the Third
Reich has been the growth of interest in *Alltagsgeschichte* (the history of
everyday life). In many respects this is an outgrowth of the 'structuralist' school, since it attempts to take the historical analysis still further
away from the political centre and towards the grassroots of society.
However, this new school of 'social history' has distanced itself from
the pioneeering work of the 'structuralists'. Instead, they have tended
to identify more closely with the philosophy of the French *Annalistes*
whose aims have been to create a more 'total' and more 'human'
history. From the early 1980s a whole range of studies have been
published which have explored the experiences of different social
groups in different regions and localities of Germany. They have
focused on all sorts of issues: sexual behaviour; the role of women;
family structure; and attitudes to death and crime. In so doing they
have broadened the methodological basis of historical research by
embracing oral history, demographical and anthropological techniques
and by exploiting computer technology for quantification. Undoubtedly, such studies have provided new and very different insights into the
Third Reich, but they have also tended to reinforce the continuity of
development argument and in the minds of some critics, to 'normalise'
the Third Reich as if it were simply any other period of German history.

3 Concluding Thoughts

Few historians would now support the view that German history made
Nazism inevitable. However, it would be equally naive to portray it as
an 'aberration', divorced from Germany's historical development and
alien to the nation. Such an interpretation would make the Nazi
retention of power for 12 years almost inexplicable. Likewise, only the
most extreme 'structuralist' would portray Hitler as a mere agent or
puppet, and even trenchant 'intentionalists' would have to accept that
Hitler alone cannot provide an adequate explanation of the Third
Reich.

So where does all this leave the poor history student? First of all it is
important to realise that there are no 'correct' conclusions to be drawn
from the various debates raised in this volume. All historical writing is
essentially a personal and provisional interpretation of the past. Howev-

er, to be good history it must examine the evidence and provide coherent explanations which are intellectually satisfying and convincing. These are the common objectives shared by academic historians and examination students. Different interpretations are more often than not a result of applying different criteria or focusing on different points of emphasis. This is why it is so important not only to read a variety of history texts, but also to talk through one's ideas with others who are studying the topic. Only then can one begin to feel comfortable with one's own point of view. What follows should be seen in this light. It is merely the interpretation of the present author. It certainly should not be viewed as definitive. It is presented in the hope that it will form a basis for further discussion.

It now seems safe to assume that the emergence of the Third Reich can be linked very clearly with several important features of Germany's past. Firstly, the regime enjoyed the backing of the country's conservative elites which had played such an central part in the nation's development since 1871. Moreover, despite the increasing radicalisation of the Nazi system that tolerance was never entirely withdrawn. Secondly, the initial thrust of Nazi foreign policy to create *Lebensraum* in the East corresponded very closely with the objectives of Imperial Germany at the start of the First World War and actually put into effect by the terms of the Treaty of Brest-Litovsk in 1918. These points represent two very important strands of continuity. However, they need to be set alongside some fundamental differences between the Third Reich and its imperial predecessor. The *Kaiserreich* did not seek to destroy the federal tradition within Germany: Nazism did. The *Kaiserreich* operated according to a constitution and its values were squarely in the tradition of what Germans call the *Rechtsstaat* (the constitutional state). Citizens enjoyed certain legal rights, which meant, for example, that only civilian courts could curtail an individual's liberty. The Third Reich, despite the 'legal revolution', behaved in a totally arbitrary fashion, which permitted (even encouraged) imprisonment without trial and state violence on a barbaric scale. As for the ideological roots of National Socialism, it is certainly true that most of its political and racial ideas, especially anti-semitism, pre-dated the Third Reich, but then there is absolutely nothing in Germany's earlier history to suggest the horrors of Auschwitz and all that it represents. The holocaust is surely on an entirely different scale to any anti-semitic precedents – it therefore marks a fundamental change rather than merely a difference in degree. Finally, although Nazi foreign policy has common links with imperial ambitions it was founded on an entirely different premise: namely that the Third Reich would create a racist utopia (a 'new order') which would eventually lead to world domination by Germany.

The emergence of the Third Reich therefore cannot be understood without drawing attention to the particular historical circumstances of

Germany. Rapid industrialisation and urbanisation had created social pressures which the conservative and authoritarian elites were unwilling to defuse by granting political reform until forced to do so by the pressures of military circumstances in 1918. Although these elites (and their political-military objectives) were to some extent eclipsed during the Weimar Republic, they were to be revived in 1933 by the alliance of many of the traditional vested interests with National Socialism. Thus, in the years 1933–45 there was certainly no fundamental social transformation and, as a result, essentially the traditional structure of society remained intact. However, there was also a crucial difference: and the difference is rooted in the vital role played by Hitler himself. Hitler's personality and ideology led to a dramatic radicalisation of policy in certain key spheres: politically, by the creation of a one-party state brutally upheld by the SS-Police-SD system, which progressively marginalised other sources of power and influence; a reorientation of society by the application of racial laws, followed by a policy of genocide; and finally, in the field of foreign policy, by the drive towards a German (Aryan) world hegemony. In this sense 1933 did mark an important turning-point, which separated it from earlier German history.

And yet, the house inherited and built by Hitler collapsed under his tutelage. By 1945 Germany as a modern nation-state had in effect ceased to exist. This was the inheritance bequeathed by Hitler's Third Reich and in that sense 1945 was an even greater turning-point. The Third Reich should be seen as a watershed in German history. It stands out in sharp relief to both the Weimar Republic and the *Kaiserreich* because, under the malign influence of Hitler, it was able to emerge and then to distort abominably certain tendencies within Germany. However, the Nazi dynamic could not be sustained and the intended new racial world order was never established. Instead, the Third Reich collapsed in an orgy of destruction which resulted in the emergence in 1945 of a Germany very different to that of 1933, 1918, 1890 or 1871.

Working on 'Conclusion: The Third Reich and German History'

This is not a chapter to make notes on in the usual fashion. Rather, it is intended to form a basis for further thought and discussion on two key issues which are inextricably linked – i) What was Nazism? and ii) How does the Third Reich fit into the broader context of German history?

The chapter describes interpretations of the Third Reich by both contemporaries and historians. They should provide a starting-point for the development of your own personal judgement.

Having read all those different views, you may feel at a bit of a loss; alternatively, you may have begun to form your own impressions. Either way, it is important that you think through the issues and clarify your thoughts so that you feel confident of arguing your case in class or in an essay. A good way to achieve this is to examine where you stand on some of the more extreme points of view. Study the following statements:

1 National Socialism was the logical outcome of German history.
2 Nazism was nothing more than Hitlerism.
3 From 1871–1945 there is a clear line of continuity in Germany's history based upon its military and socio-economic structure.
4 The Third Reich was an aberration in both European and German history.
5 Nazism was merely the German expression of European fascism.

In the case of each point of view you should do the following:
a) Refer back to the notes made on earlier chapters.
b) Re-read the final section of chapters 3, 4, 5, 6 and 7.
c) Make a list of all the points, ideas and facts to support the statement and all those to counter it.
d) Write a 100 word assessment of the point of view.

These paragraphs have been written with the assumption that students are not only well versed in the history of the Third Reich, but also have a working knowledge of earlier German history and other aspects of twentieth-century European history. This is because you can only fully appreciate any topic of history if you understand its context. It is also because some of the real 'joys' of history come from assessing similarities and differences or continuity and change. You may not feel ready to tackle these tasks until you are nearing the end of your course and have gained that broader perspective. However, at some point you will need to confront the big issues. It will not be easy, but it is what real history is all about and it will stand you in very good stead for your examination.

Answering essay questions on 'Conclusion: The Third Reich and German History'

You should *not* read this section until you have thoroughly worked through the above section.

Study the following essay questions:

1 Compare and contrast the regimes of Hitler and Mussolini.
2 Is it accurate to describe both Hitler's Germany and Stalin's Russia as 'totalitarian'?
3 Is it incorrect to define Nazism as Germany's fascism?

All these essays are 'comparison' questions. Even question 3 falls into this category because it can be answered only by reference to fascism in general. Such questions are not easy. You should tackle them only if you have a good general understanding of all the regimes implied in the question. You also need the ability to organise that knowledge with flexibility and clarity (and if you're in the examination room all this has to be done quite quickly).

How do you tackle such questions? Certainly, you must not write an essay of two halves, because that will prevent effective analysis of the similarities and differences. Instead, it is important that you plan a structure which will encourage comparison throughout. Look at question 1 and complete a matrix such as the one below:

	Hitler's Germany	Mussolini's Italy	Assessment
Structure of regime			
Economic policy			
Ideology			
Foreign policy			
Social policy			

As you can see there is a massive amount of material to exploit. It is therefore vital to plan well if you are really going to analyse effectively. By taking a thematic approach you create a clear structure whilst also alluding to the similarities and differences all the time. When you have completed a thorough plan and written out a conclusion in full, try a similar approach with question 2.

Chronological Table

1918	Nov.	Surrender of Germany in First World War. Abdication of Kaiser. Declaration of republic.
1920	Feb.	NSDAP 25-point party programme drawn up.
1923	8 Nov.	Beer Hall *putsch* in Munich: disastrous fiasco.
1924		Hitler in Landsberg prison. *Mein Kampf* written.
1925	27 Feb.	NSDAP refounded.
1926	Feb.	Bamberg conference: Hitler's leadership of party re-established.
1929	Oct.	Death of Gustav Stresemann. Wall Street Crash.
	Dec.	National referendum on Young Plan.
1930	Mar.	Collapse of Müller's coalition government. Appointment of Brüning as Chancellor.
	Sept.	*Reichstag* election: Nazis emerged as second largest party.
1932	Apr.	Re-election of Hindenburg as President.
	May	Resignation of Brüning. Papen became Chancellor.
	July	*Reichstag* election: Nazis by far the largest party.
	13 Aug.	Hitler's demand to head a new government rejected by Hindenburg.
	Nov.	*Reichstag* election.
	Dec.	Resignation of Papen. Appointment of Schleicher as Chancellor.
1933	30 Jan.	Hitler appointed Chancellor.
	27 Feb.	*Reichstag* fire: Communists blamed.
	5 Mar.	Last elections according to Weimar constitution.
	23 Mar.	Enabling Act passed.
	1 Apr.	Boycott of Jewish shops.
	2 May	Dissolution of free trade unions.
	14 July	All political opposition to NSDAP declared illegal.
	14 Oct.	Germany withdrew from League of Nations and Disarmament Conference.
1934	26 Jan.	Non-aggression pact signed with Poland.
	30 June	Night of the Long Knives: destruction of SA by SS.
	2 Aug.	Death of Hindenburg: Hitler assumed the combined offices of Chancellor and President. Oath of loyalty taken by army.
1935	13 Jan.	Return of Saar.
	16 Mar.	Reintroduction of military conscription.
	18 June	Anglo-German Naval Agreement.
	15 Sept.	Nuremberg Race Laws.
1936	7 Mar.	Re-militarisation of Rhineland by German troops.

	26 July	Start of German intervention in Spanish Civil War.
	9 Sept.	Introduction of 'Four Year Plan'.
	25 Oct.	German-Italian rapprochement – Rome-Berlin Axis.
1937	5 Nov.	Hitler's address to chiefs of armed services – the so-called Hossbach Conference.
	26 Nov.	Resignation of Schacht as Economics Minister: control of economy passed to Göring.
1938	4 Feb.	Dismissal of Blomberg. Neurath replaced by Ribbentrop as Foreign Minister.
	12 Mar.	*Anschluss* with Austria.
	Sept.	Sudeten crisis.
	30 Sept.	Munich agreement ceded Sudeteneland to Germany.
	9 Nov.	*Kristallnacht*. Organised pogrom against Jews.
1939	15 Mar.	Invasion of Czechoslovakia: Munich agreement undone and self-determination ignored.
	22 May	Pact of Steel – German-Italian military alliance.
	23 Aug.	Nazi-Soviet Pact.
	1 Sept.	German invasion of Poland.
	3 Sept.	British and French declaration of war.
1940	9 Apr.	German invasion of Denmark and Norway.
	10 May	German invasion of Low Countries and France.
	Sept.	Luftwaffe failed to win Battle of Britain.
1941	6 Apr.	German invasion of Greece and Yugoslavia.
	10 May	Flight of Rudolf Hess to Scotland: Bormann assumed control of Party apparatus.
	22 June	'Operation Barbarossa' – German invasion of USSR. *Einsatzgruppen* started operations.
	Dec.	Advance of German troops halted before Moscow.
	11 Dec.	German declaration of war on USA following Pearl Harbor: continental war 'globalised'.
1942	20 Jan.	Wannsee conference: 'Final Solution' to Jewish problem agreed upon.
	8 Feb.	Death of Fritz Todt, Minister for Armaments: his successor, Albert Speer, geared arms production to the demands of 'total war'.
	3 Nov.	British victory at El Alamein.
1943	31 Jan.	German surrender at Stalingrad.
	18 Feb.	Declaration of 'total war' by Goebbels.
	10 June	Anglo-American saturation bombing begun.
1944	6 June	Allied landings in Normandy.
	20 July	Stauffenberg bomb plot: failure resulted in brutal recriminations. Thorough purge of army.
1945	Jan.	Russian troops advanced into Prussia.
	30 Apr.	Hitler's suicide.
	7 May	German surrender: division of Germany.

Glossary

Anschluss	Union of Germany and Austria.
Bekennende Kirche	Confessional Church. Protestant churchmen opposed to Nazi interference in the church.
BDM	Bund Deutscher Mädel – League of German Girls.
Blitzkrieg	Lightning war. Military strategy to achieve rapid advance by use of motorised infantry, tanks and air-bombardment.
DAF	Deutsche Arbeitsfront – German Labour Front. Nazi organisation of workers.
Deutsche Christen	German Christians. Protestants who aimed to reconcile Christianity and National Socialism.
DFW	Deutsches Frauenwerk – German Women's Enterprise. Nazi women's organisation.
Diktat	Right-wing description of Versailles treaty. Literally, a 'dictated' peace.
Einsatzgruppen	Action squads. SS units responsible for the murder of inferior racial groups.
Führer	Leader.
Führerprinzip	The leadership principle.
Gau	Region. The basis of Nazi Party organisation.
Gauleiter	Regional Party leader.
Gestapo	Geheime Staatspolizei – secret state police.
Gleichschaltung	Co-ordination. Nazi policy of establishing effective centralised control.
Historikerstreit	Historians' dispute. Academic dispute amongst Germany's historians from 1986.
Herrenvolk	Master-race.
HJ	Hitler Jugend – Hitler Youth.
Junker	Prussian landowner.
Kaiser	Emperor.
Kaiserreich	Imperial Germany 1871–1918.
KDF	Kraft durch Freude – Strength through Joy. Nazi organisation for workers' recreation.
Kinder, Küche, Kirche	Children, Kitchen, Church. Slogan encouraging women to stay at home.
Kreis	District.
Kristallnacht	Crystal night. Pogrom of November 1938.
Kulturkampf	Cultural struggle. Bismarck's anti-Catholic policy of the 1870s.
Landtag	Provincial parliament.

Lebensborn	Literally 'Spring of Life'. Nazi organisation to care for unmarried (Aryan) mothers.
Lebensraum	Living-space. Policy of expansion.
Luftwaffe	Air-force.
Mein Kampf	My Struggle. Hitler's autobiography and political exposition (1924).
Mit Brennender Sorge	With Burning Concern. Papal encyclical of 1937 critical of Nazism.
Mittelstand	Middle class. Traditionally referred to the artisan/shopkeeper rather than the new industrial entrepreneur.
Napolas	Elite schools.
NSDAP	Nationalsozialistische Deutsche Arbeiterpartei – National Socialist German Workers' Party.
NSF	Nationalsozialistische Frauenschaft – National Socialist Womanhood.
NSLB	Nationalsozialistische Lehrer Bund – National Socialist Teachers' League.
OKW	Oberkommando der Wehrmacht – High Command of the Armed Forces. Created in 1938 to bring forces under Hitler's control.
Ordensburgen	Elite schools.
Putsch	Coup or revolt.
Rechtsstaat	Constitutional state. State based upon the rule of law.
Reich	Empire.
Reichsrat	Second chamber of German parliament, representing federal provinces.
Reichstag	Representative chamber of parliament.
Reichsstatthalter	Reich Commissioners. Appointed in 1933 to oversee Nazi take-over of federal provinces.
SA	Sturm Abteilung – Stormtroopers.
SS	Schutz Staffeln – Protection squad.
Stahlhelm	Steel Helmet. Para-military organisation of veterans. Right-wing.
Stufenplan	Gradual plan. Theory that Hitler's foreign policy was set to follow a number of stages.
Volk	A people/nation with ethnic and cultural identities.
Völkischer Beobachter	People's Observer. Nazi newspaper.
Volksgemeinschaft	People's community. Nazi concept of national integration based upon race.
Wehrwirtschaft	Defence economy. Theory that the German economy should be geared in peacetime to the needs of war.

Further Reading

Textbooks

Because of the importance of this topic in German and European history it would be worthwhile looking at several general textbooks. You should not make detailed notes on them, but you should try to understand how the author sees the Third Reich in the broader context. By far the most accessible of the many general histories of Germany is:
William Carr, *A History of Germany 1815–1990* (Edward Arnold 4th ed. 1992)
This is a thorough but readable survey, which highlights the differing historical interpretations.

More intellectually demanding are:
Volker Berghahn, *Modern Germany* (CUP 2nd ed. 1987)
Gordon Craig, *Germany 1866–1945* (OUP 1981)
The emphasis and approach of the two books is entirely different. It would be a good idea to see if you can detect these differences by dipping into one or two of the relevant chapters of each book.

Biographies

There are numerous biographies of Hitler. However, many are sensationalist and populist in style. Academic historians have tended to fight shy of the biographical approach because they are only too aware of its inadequacies in explaining the Third Reich as a whole. Another reason might be that the very first major biography, published as long ago as 1952, still shows no sign of being superseded. This is:
Alan Bullock, *Hitler. A Study in Tyranny* (Penguin 1962)
This book remains a historical classic. It is an excellent example of how good academic history can be written in an easy-going style. In particular, read chapters 3–5, which consider the rise to power and the creation of the dictatorship, and chapter 7, which shows how a good biographer actually gets inside the mind of his subject

The one other Hitler-centred book you should try to look at is:
Ian Kershaw, *The 'Hitler Myth'* (OUP 1987)
Written by one of Britain's leading experts on Nazi Germany, it tries to put Hitler's role in the Third Reich into perspective by examining the propagandist image and the political reality.

If you want to find out about other leading Nazis the best place to start is:
Joachim Fest, *The Face of the Third Reich* (Penguin 1977)

Historiographical Reviews

By far the best general survey of the controversies surrounding Nazi Germany is:
Ian Kershaw, *The Nazi Dictatorship. Problems and Perspectives of Interpretation* (Edward Arnold 2nd ed. 1989)
However, although it is well-organised, so that each chapter considers a separate area of controversy, it is not an easy read and you will have to take it slowly and think critically about the ideas raised. If you can persevere, you will be well rewarded.
Alternatively, you could look at part two of:
Klaus Hildebrand, *The Third Reich* (Allen & Unwin 1984)
This is shorter and slightly easier to read.

Specialist Studies

If you wish to study some of the historical controversies more deeply you will need to select your reading with great care. The academic literature on the Third Reich is enormous and much of it is detailed and very specialised. The following are suggested 'starting-points' for various aspects of the topic:

a) Rise to Power
Peter D. Stachura (ed.), *The Nazi Machtergreifung* (London 1983)
W.S. Allen, *The Nazi Seizure of Power: The Experience of a Single Town* (Eyre & Spottiswoode 1966)
Jeremy Noakes, 'Nazi Voters' in *History Today* (August 1980)

b) Structure of the Regime
Karl Dietrich Bracher, *The German Dictatorship* (Penguin 1973)

c) Society and Economy
R. Grunberger, *A Social History of the Third Reich* (Penguin 1974)
R. Overy, *The Nazi Economic Recovery 1932–1938* (London 1982)

d) Foreign Policy
William Carr, *Arms, Autarky and Aggression* (London 2nd ed. 1979)
Klaus Hildebrand, *The Third Reich* (Allen & Unwin 1984)

Sources

For the definitive collection of documents in English refer to:
J. Noakes & G. Pridham (ed.), *Nazism 1919–1945* 3 Vols. (Exeter 1983)
For a more select collection of sources and also a range of pictorial material look at:
J. Laver *Nazi Germany 1933–1945* (Hodder & Stoughton 1991)

Index